More Praise for *Life Entrepreneurs*

"The real question is not how to just make a living, but how to make a life. *Life Entrepreneurs* helps all who are struggling to integrate money and meaning in their careers to do just that."
— Dr. Mark S. Albion, *New York Times* best-selling author of *Making a Life, Making a Living,* and *True to Yourself*

"Highly effective people take a principled, integrated approach to life—inspired by vision and implemented with persistence. Gergen and Vanourek do a wonderful job bringing this philosophy to life through colorful storytelling and a well-conceived framework. Pick up this book and read it. It might change your life."
— Stephen R. Covey, best-selling author of *The 7 Habits of Highly Effective People* and *The 8th Habit: From Effectiveness to Greatness*

"Gergen and Vanourek provide a great road map for anyone who is looking to find success and fulfillment doing what they are passionate about."
— Steve Ells, founder, chairman, and CEO, Chipotle Mexican Grill

"Like jazz musicians, good entrepreneurs improvise, finding the roads less traveled. *Life Entrepreneurs* does a great job of capturing this spirit and sharing valuable lessons for work and life."
— Gary Erickson, owner/founder, Clif Bar & Company; author of *Raising the Bar*

"*Life Entrepreneurs* captures the essence of the Creative Age, where people are the true source of economic growth."
— Richard Florida, best-selling author of *Rise of the Creative Class*; director, Martin Prosperity Institute, Rotman School of Management

"In *Life Entrepreneurs*, Christopher Gergen and Gregg Vanourek address the central issue of every emerging leader, 'How can I design my life to be both fulfilling and significant?' Through the life stories of many entrepreneurs who are impacting the world in dramatic ways, this compelling and refreshing new book provides deep insights that make it a must-read for all of us to use on our own journeys."
— Bill George, author of *True North* and *Authentic Leadership*; former chairman and CEO, Medtronic

"At last, a powerful guide to integrating life, work, purpose, and work-life balance—one of the greatest needs of leaders in all three sectors of the emerging work force. Christopher and Gregg bring a new definition, a new clarity to life entrepreneurship that will make a difference in the lives of leaders at every level. A great gift."
— Frances Hesselbein, chairman, Leader to Leader Institute; former CEO, Girl Scouts of America

"*Life Entrepreneurs* is wonderfully written, highly engaging, and inspiring. As people who aspire to be an 'entrepreneurial couple,' we found Gergen's and Vanourek's book full of thoughtful insights and powerful strategic advice on how to live a life that integrates and balances family, friends, work, and personal fulfillment. The authors demonstrate how anyone can become a life entrepreneur. This book is a gift for all of us."

—Alan Khazei, co-founder, City Year Inc., and Vanessa Kirsch, president and founder, New Profit, Inc.

"This is provocative reading for all those committed to creating a life of significance and meaning. Filled with helpful strategies and hopeful stories, *Life Entrepreneurs* is an intriguing, challenging guide for the next generation of leaders."

—Wendy Kopp, president and founder, Teach for America

"Our work and life can be a great adventure, an opportunity to serve people in compelling and meaningful ways. In this book, we gain powerful insights on how to realize those important possibilities."

—Linda Mason, chairman and co-founder, Bright Horizons Family Solutions

"Gergen and Vanourek offer a fresh and vital approach to life and career planning. The book speaks directly to the younger generations of Americans who increasingly reject pigeon-holed and segmented careers but, instead, are choosing to create integrated lives filled with, 'passion, connection, and significance.' I highly recommend this book to anyone who is seeking The Good Life."

—James O'Toole, author of *Creating the Good Life*; former executive vice president, Aspen Institute

"Gergen and Vanourek have done a spectacular job shining a light on a new approach to professional success and personal fulfillment: the life entrepreneur. With dozens of inspiring profiles and page after page of smart advice, this book belongs on the nightstand of every thoughtful businessperson in America."

—Daniel H. Pink, *New York Times* best-selling author of *A Whole New Mind* and *Free Agent Nation*

"*Life Entrepreneurs* offers a new way of thinking about life and work, and a window into the future. I highly recommend it."

—Robert Reich, former U.S. Secretary of Labor

"Business leaders and entrepreneurs alike will greatly benefit from *Life Entrepreneurs*. It captures the essential qualities of leadership including finding a worthy path, being willing to fail, and taking courageous action. I highly recommend it."

—Howard Schultz, chairman, Starbucks Coffee Company

"This book is true, smart, honest, hopeful, and helpful. It is essential reading for anyone who shares the belief that work and life aren't two separate categories, divided by pain, pressure, and a paycheck. Instead, here's the good news: entrepreneurship isn't just a way of making a living—it's a way of life. Buy this book, read it, and then do it!"

—Alan M. Webber, co-founding editor, *Fast Company* magazine; former editorial director, *Harvard Business Review*

LIFE ENTREPRENEURS

Warren Bennis

A WARREN BENNIS BOOK

This collection of books is devoted exclusively to new and exemplary contributions to management thought and practice. The books in this series are addressed to thoughtful leaders, executives, and managers of all organizations who are struggling with and committed to responsible change. My hope and goal is to spark new intellectual capital by sharing ideas positioned at an angle to conventional thought—in short, to publish books that disturb the present in the service of a better future.

Books in the Warren Bennis Signature Series

LIFE
ENTREPRENEURS

Ordinary People Creating Extraordinary Lives

Christopher Gergen

Gregg Vanourek

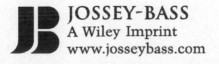

JOSSEY-BASS
A Wiley Imprint
www.josseybass.com

Published by Jossey-Bass
A Wiley Imprint
989 Market Street, San Francisco, CA 94103-1741—www.josseybass.com

Readers should be aware that Internet Web sites offered as citations and/or sources for further
information may have changed or disappeared between the time this was written and when it is read.

Limit of Liability/Disclaimer of Warranty: While the publisher and author have used their best efforts
in preparing this book, they make no representations or warranties with respect to the accuracy
or completeness of the contents of this book and specifically disclaim any implied warranties of
merchantability or fitness for a particular purpose. No warranty may be created or extended by sales
representatives or written sales materials. The advice and strategies contained herein may not be
suitable for your situation. You should consult with a professional where appropriate. Neither the
publisher nor author shall be liable for any loss of profit or any other commercial damages, including
but not limited to special, incidental, consequential, or other damages.

Jossey-Bass books and products are available through most bookstores. To contact Jossey-Bass directly
call our Customer Care Department within the U.S. at 800-956-7739, outside the U.S. at 317-572-3986,
or fax 317-572-4002.

Jossey-Bass also publishes its books in a variety of electronic formats. Some content that appears in
print may not be available in electronic books.

Library of Congress Cataloging-in-Publication Data

Gergen, Christopher, 1970-
    Life entrepreneurs : ordinary people creating extraordinary lives / Christopher Gergen,
Gregg Vanourek.
        p.   cm.
    Includes bibliographical references and index.
    ISBN 978-0-7879-8862-3 (cloth)
        1. Creative ability in business.   2. Entrepreneurship.   3. Work and family.
4. Maturation (Psychology)   I. Vanourek, Gregg.   II.   Title.
HD53.G47 2008
650.1—dc22
                                                                2007049549

Printed in the United States of America

FIRST EDITION
HB Printing 10 9 8 7 6 5 4

Contents

From Christopher:
To Heather and Maya (Team Daddy)
and to Mom and Dad—my roots and wings

From Gregg:
To Alexandra, enamored with life
and awash in possibility

FOREWORD

Usually in business books that tackle the notion of entrepreneurship, there is the unspoken (and sometimes spoken) assumption that to be an entrepreneur, you have to give 110 percent to your work at the expense of other aspects of your life. These authors focus on how to create extraordinary organizations, while ignoring the balance and quality of the entrepreneur's life as a whole. But our legacy is so much more than the bottom line.

What I love about this book is that Christopher Gergen and Gregg Vanourek have turned that proposition on its head. Both have succeeded as entrepreneurs—in business, education, nonprofits, and more—but at pivotal moments in their lives, each wondered whether they had been channeling their energy and attention into the right things. What they realized is that by turning their entrepreneurial spirit toward other aspects of their lives, they could create something extraordinary and much more fulfilling, both personally and professionally.

This is one of the most inspiring and unique books I have come across in a long time. It addresses many of the most daunting dilemmas that modern workers, especially those under fifty, face: How can I achieve meaning, personal growth, and happiness? How can I impact the world and other people in a positive way? Can I overcome my fears and challenge the status quo to become the person I feel I should be? And on top of it all, how can I find the time and the means to answer these questions while trying to make a living?

The authors deserve much credit for addressing these issues in a totally novel way, one that not only instructs but entertains. Their concept of "Life Entrepreneurship" is a deep one. Not only have they done firsthand research by finding fascinating, real-life entrepreneurs to share their stories, they have also asked difficult questions and distilled their commonalities so that the rest of us can start to examine our paths as well, at any age and place in life.

And this book couldn't come at a better time. The world has rarely needed capable leaders more than it does now, and this need goes far beyond the boardroom. We need it in terms of family, community, and social responsibility. *Life Entrepreneurs* cuts right to the essence of leadership in that it seeks to integrate all of these and encourages us to align our values with everything we do and take responsibility for every facet of our lives.

But above all, life entrepreneurship is an adventure. It doesn't just arise from need, but from desire—to be something more, to create something new, to explore beyond the usual boundaries. It's an appeal to all of us to become our best selves. As the authors say, the opportunities for challenge, contribution, and fulfillment are there; we just have to grab them.

Warren Bennis
Santa Monica, California
November 2007

INTRODUCTION

The idea for this book came to us one warm spring afternoon in Virginia, as we sat on a picnic bench with an intriguing question: *How can we create extraordinary lives?*

As we wrestled with this question, we drew on a source of mutual inspiration—the power of creating innovative new enterprises. We are both entrepreneurs. Between us, we have started or helped to start companies, non-profits, schools, a foundation, a national government initiative, and even a live music café in South America. We wondered if that entrepreneurial approach could be applied to our lives.

As we sat and talked, our lives were at crossroads. Gregg was reclaiming his life after a start-up experience that was both thrilling and punishing. After helping to build a fledgling venture into a national education enterprise, he was eager to take a new direction in life, one definitively of his own choosing. Christopher was ready to pursue a new challenge after cofounding an online tutoring company that serves students globally. Both of us were starting families and were committed to embracing and upholding that awesome responsibility.

Under the hot Virginia sun, we discussed how our penchant for creating new ventures might fit into the context of our lives. Could we apply the entrepreneurial mind-set of opportunity recognition, vision creation, innovation, and initiative to create a better life? Could we creatively design a life aligned with our values? Could we lead our lives in such a way that our work, life, and purpose would be not only balanced but integrated?

The questions were provocative and disquieting. We sensed that the answers carried significant implications for how we could live.

In pursuit of understanding, we reflected on our own experiences and conducted research in the fields of entrepreneurship, leadership, and personal development. Mostly, though, we listened to others. In the end, we went out and interviewed fifty-five business and social entrepreneurs, all of whom brought a certain amount of entrepreneurial flair to their lives as well as their work. Nearly all come from ordinary backgrounds, yet they have created extraordinary lives for themselves and those around them through a mix of drive and direction. You have probably heard of some of their organizations: Starbucks, Chipotle, Cranium, Clif Bar, RealNetworks, Hanna Andersson, KIPP (the Knowledge Is Power Program), Share Our Strength, and perhaps others. The people we interviewed range from prominent figures to less well-known folks, from business, non-profit, and political leaders to chefs, musicians, journalists, professors, and ministers—even a rancher, a fighter pilot, and a yoga instructor. Their professional accomplishments are exceptional, but what really differentiates them is the way they have led entrepreneurial lives—on their terms and aligned with their values and priorities.

In the course of these interviews, we sought to learn about the people behind the enterprises: Who are they? What makes them tick? Who influenced them? Why and how did they make the decisions they did? What mistakes have they made? What have they learned? What advice do they have for others?

Their answers are important because they show how entrepreneurial principles can be applied to life. These are lessons that hold promise for all of us, not just those who have started an enterprise or hung out a shingle. In many ways, we consider this cohort of fifty-five to be pioneers of living in today's world—harbingers of what the future might hold in store.

For us, the interview process was powerful. It deepened our understanding of the issues, challenges, struggles, and strategies of entrepreneurs. It forced us to look closely at our own life decisions and often left us inspired. In their stories, we found incredible examples of passion, courage, integrity, perseverance, and service.

When transcriptions of these interviews were compiled—altogether about a thousand pages of text—powerful themes were sounded, like a chorus of voices converging in unscripted harmony. Here are some of the major patterns we spotted:

- All of the entrepreneurs we interviewed made a conscious decision to walk their own path and forge their own future—often going against prevailing expectations.

- There was a direct correlation between the purposefulness and conviction with which they walk their path in life and the passion and joy they feel for their life and work.
- Many of them don't think of themselves as dividing their time between "work" and "life." For many, these are integrated, not compartmentalized, pursuits. They are creating, owning, and taking responsibility for every facet of their lives with an integrated approach.
- Their dispositions toward risk were all over the map—ranging from those who were somewhat risk-averse to a few intrepid "risk junkies." But they were *all* willing to take measured risks in pursuit of a worthy project or goal. They saw risk as an inherent part of life and took steps to mitigate it through thoughtful planning and disciplined execution.
- All of them have experienced failure and dealt with significant setbacks. Many have encountered life-changing episodes of tragedy, illness, loss, financial difficulty, and more.
- Several found great value in stepping off the path to renew, recharge, and sometimes reinvent their lives, discovering that periods of activity and achievement must be counterbalanced with periods of rest and regrouping.
- Their life path was usually a winding one, not linear. In most cases, it made much more sense looking backward. As they moved forward, they were both shaping the future and responding to it.
- Most of them came to the conclusion that it's not all about them—far from it. They have cultivated healthy support systems, and many have become deeply connected, civic-minded leaders.

From these interviews and our research and experiences, we conclude that leading life in an entrepreneurial manner can be what tips our lives from ordinary to extraordinary. Moreover, it directly addresses a number of challenges currently facing our society. As such, this approach has the potential to transform not only individual lives but also the culture of our workplaces, the dynamics of our communities, and the attitudes and behaviors of rising generations of leaders. Let's be clear: this approach to life is not solely for business and social entrepreneurs. It is a path that is available to all who choose it as a strategy to improve and transform lives.

We are both in our midthirties, part of a "seeking" generation navigating a rapidly changing world and searching for a better way to live. Our experiences, research, and interviews have shown us that there is an emerging trend among rising generations, one of rejecting past approaches to stable careers, job security, and lives built around safety, security, and status. In their place, we are seeing more and more people building their lives around passion, connection, and significance.

This approach is filling a growing need among generations of young people eager to find and sound their own voice in today's world in the hope of improving it. This approach is also becoming a new model for learning, leading, living, and serving. As such, we believe that now is the time to name this emerging phenomenon, define it, and draw out its lessons and implications. We call it *life entrepreneurship:* creating a life of significance through opportunity recognition, innovation, and action.

An entrepreneurial life tracks the rhythms of start-ups: identifying a need, recognizing an opportunity, creating a vision, developing a plan, building a support network, taking action, mitigating risk, adapting to challenges, evaluating progress, making adjustments, and cycling through the process again.

We believe that entrepreneurship is not solely the province of the professional. It is a mind-set, approach, and process that can be applied to any endeavor—including that of leading our lives. In the same way that a business or social entrepreneur creates an enterprise through artful combinations of vision, creativity, dynamism, and risk, so too can we—any one of us—build an extraordinary life. We can fashion a life that is purposeful, self-directed, and aligned with who we truly are—providing us with opportunities for challenge, contribution, and fulfillment.

The central thesis of this book is this: the path to a better life for growing numbers of people today is to apply the principles of entrepreneurship to life itself. Those principles were developed and honed in the business world and have migrated to the civic sector. Increasingly it is becoming clear that, when applied to our lives, they can be catalytic and positively transformative.

Although this approach is being embraced by younger generations (and may be part of our lasting legacy), it is not confined to us. The trend transcends barriers of age, gender, and nationality.

We will see this in the pages that follow, with life entrepreneurs in their twenties and others in their sixties, from Montana to New Jersey to Brazil and South Africa.

This book is about how to lead an entrepreneurial life—discovering what we call our *core identity*, envisioning the good life, and taking action to pursue it with all the grit and vigor we can muster. It illustrates life entrepreneurship through an actionable framework and stories of fifty-five extraordinary people who have blazed these trails. We wrote this book to help people lead meaningful and significant lives. It is for a wide-ranging audience, including emerging leaders and budding entrepreneurs; those interested in entrepreneurial leadership, personal development, and community building; and those contemplating or experiencing a life or career change, facing a challenge or crisis, or starting to think about their legacy.

Books about life and how to live it are not meant for small niches. This book is different from most leadership and business books because it takes an integrated approach to work and life, recognizing that these converge. It is different from most personal development books because it draws on entrepreneurship as a catalyst for extraordinary lives. And it draws heavily on the unique, real-world stories of fifty-five people who have found success in life and work.

This book is necessary because there are many common traps that we fall into as we navigate our lives. Many of us walk a path in life that others have chosen for us, letting others dictate our career, choices, and fate. Others stick with the first path they come upon, doggedly committing to a career or profession that may not be a good fit with their values and aspirations. We compartmentalize our work and life with artificial distinctions and with no expectation that two could be integrated. We fall prey to burnout that comes from information overload, perpetual busyness, and racing against the clock. We fail to plan with our whole lives in mind, consumed by the pressing obligations of the day. We defer our dreams to a distant and precarious future through rationalizations and compromise. We give too much weight to the aspects of our lives that are material, tangible, and productized at the expense of those that are personal, interconnected, and lasting. And we "cocoon" at home or in the office when we could be engaging with our neighbors and communities. This book provides a road map for how we can get back on track.

Although the book addresses the challenges many people face in navigating an abundance of choices, we also recognize that there are too many people today with a dearth of choices. In that respect, this book is a call to arms to be part of the solution by helping to expand opportunities for others. Even as we live the best lives we are capable of, we can also choose to use our energy, talent, and resources to contribute to our communities and those who have less. For those who might view life entrepreneurship only as a luxury of the well-to-do, we call their attention to what Henry David Thoreau called our ability to elevate our condition through conscious endeavor—a gift that is universally available, though admittedly more difficult in unfavorable circumstances. Some might choose skepticism, but we are inclined to place our bet on the fortitude and resourcefulness of the human spirit.

The premise behind this book is that we all have the potential to be life entrepreneurs—and when we choose to be purposeful, creative, and dynamic leaders of our own lives, we strengthen our relationships, increase our happiness, and enhance our ability to make a difference in our families, workplaces, community, and beyond.

Emerging generations of leaders are finding that we don't fit neatly into life's categories of professions, trades, and beaten paths. There is so much we want for our work and lives that transcends those conventions. We are rejecting the prospect of being slotted into prescribed "lifetime jobs"; instead, we are embracing multisector, multifaceted careers. We strive to make lasting contributions to worthy fields (such as business, technology, education, health care, poverty reduction, and the environment), but we recognize there are many means to accomplish these ends. We are willing to work hard, but we are wary of work without authenticity or potential for measurable impact.

For too many, our long march of jobs has been divorced from the larger context of what we want in our lives and how we can best put our talents to use for others. Where can we go to figure out what we want for the *whole* of our lives? How can we start building a life that integrates family, health, career, friendship, community, learning, and other priorities in *practical* ways?

There is an urgency to these questions. Currently, too many of us buy into the false dichotomy of either paying the rent or leading a life of fulfillment, reluctant to believe the two can go together. The unhappy result is an existence of compromise. Today, about 6 percent of people in the U.S. call themselves "very happy"—a number that has declined since 1950.[1] Psychologist Edward Deiner, who has spent his career studying happiness, has noted that the average score on a test of life satisfaction in the U.S. is "slightly satisfied." Nearly 25 percent of U.S. employees are dissatisfied with their jobs, and only 14 percent of employees are very satisfied with them.[2] These data points are similar in other countries and cultures.

Part of the problem is that we are overly concerned with how we stack up against others, and we are becoming hyper-individualistic. Although record numbers of people are working for themselves, they often do it by staring into a computer screen. We are cocooning ourselves into oversized houses and oversized cars with an ever-growing array of technological gadgets. In our world of 24×7 connectivity, we are less connected to our communities. We are running harder, working longer, and earning more, but to what end? It has left us, as philosopher William James put it, only "half-awake"—sleepwalking through life, blind to the opportunities that surround us.

Looking at the big picture, we face widening economic disparity; global poverty, hunger, and disease; business and political corruption scandals; climate change; and more. People are beginning to wake up and realize that the traditional ways of living and leading are not working. Existing institutions are not sufficient, and our current ways of thinking are not up to the task.

We can do something. By taking responsibility for our lives and the challenges in our communities, we can turn helplessness into hopefulness. This sense of personal ownership and accountability allows us to approach our lives in a way that is good both for our own well-being and for the community at large. When we have the courage to pursue possibilities and solutions with vision, passion, and persistence, our lives take on new significance and the joy of living is unparalleled.

In his groundbreaking book *Authentic Happiness,* Martin Seligman, one of the forefathers of the positive psychology movement, points to research that happiness is derived from three factors:

1. *Pleasure* (the "whatever makes you feel good" variety)
2. *Engagement* (the depth of involvement in family, work, romance, and hobbies)
3. *Meaning* (using personal strengths to serve some larger end)

Of the three, pleasure is the most fleeting and least consequential. As Seligman points out, "This is newsworthy because so many Americans build their lives around pursuing pleasure. It turns out that engagement and meaning are much more important."[3] Our interviews and personal experiences bear this out.

Take, for example, the time that Christopher decided to leave a blossoming career as a writer for *Headline News* at the Cable News Network (CNN) to spend a year traveling solo through Latin America. He had gone to work for CNN—a stable, responsible job coming out of college—mostly because it was expected of him. The job had prestige, and it was an easy thing to explain to his parents and their friends. In "keeping up with the Joneses," he was making all the right moves. But it wasn't him. Although the job was rich in intellectual stimulation, the passion wasn't there. So, against the advice of all, he gathered his savings and headed south.

He ended up in Santiago, Chile, where he landed a job with a television network developing distance education programming. There he quickly noticed that, although Santiago had more than two dozen universities and every plaza was filled with young people painting or playing a guitar, there was no creative place to bring all this energy together. With a passion for art and music and nothing to lose, he started exploring what it would take to create such a space—a cultural gathering spot for young bohemians where Chile's fine wines could be poured to the sound of live music and theater every night.

He shared this vision with a group of local artists and actors he had met during his travels, and they embraced the idea. His adrenaline flowed as the idea grew from the proverbial sketch on a napkin into a full-fledged community effort. Despite the fact that none of the original partners had any experience starting or running a restaurant or bar—or any business, for that matter—the concept gained momentum. After several months of seeking funding, they raised $40,000 from local investors. Soon after, a four-thousand-square-foot Victorian mansion near the artistic neighborhood of Plaza Ñuñoa was transformed into an eighty-seat restaurant, rotating art gallery, bar, and theater featuring live music, one-act plays, and film seven nights a week.

Christopher had never felt more alive. As he biked through the city to the café, he was fully awake to life's possibilities. By choosing to leave Atlanta and take his own path in life—one against the grain of professional and parental expectations—he found that new doors were being flung open and new relationships were flourishing.

One of these friendships was with a university president who had started his own college with just two classrooms and fifty students. Within five years, it had ballooned to five thousand students. When asked what he called himself, he replied, "*Un empresario cultural*"—a cultural entrepreneur.

Though Christopher had never considered himself an entrepreneur, here was a person doing with his life just what Christopher dreamed of: taking a big idea and making it happen in the service of others. That day, Christopher made a promise to himself that he too would become a cultural entrepreneur and use his entrepreneurial passions to create new learning environments for others.

He made good on that promise, eventually returning to the States, selling the café, solidifying his knowledge base and plans in graduate school, and launching a number of for-profit and non-profit education ventures.

Today, Christopher is still trying to bring an entrepreneurial mind-set to life. By remaining focused on who he is and seeking opportunities aligned with this spirit, he met his life partner, got married on a faraway island, took a two-month honeymoon in Africa, created a new company with a great business partner and a flexible schedule to prioritize parenthood (and align his work with his passions and values), traveled the world with his family, found his way back to teaching, and embarked on this book project.

In fact, Christopher has discovered that when the entrepreneurial mind-set is not brought into life's decisions, the result is often misdirection, stress, and regret.

These were the experiences and perspectives that Christopher brought to the conversation with Gregg on that spring afternoon in Virginia.

Gregg too was turning his focus to who he was and where he wanted to be going. In college, he had been challenged by a remarkable professor, John Roth, not only to ask the big questions in life, but to *live* them, and by a course that exposed students to centuries of thinking on how to create "the good life." It was Gregg's first awakening to the power of living purposefully, examining what it is we hope to do with our days, and he found the possibilities intoxicating.

After graduate school in London, he took on a series of entrepreneurial challenges in the Washington, D.C., area, including helping to launch a national foundation and an educational scholarship program for children living in poverty, coauthoring a book on public charter schools, helping to build a start-up education company into a national market leader, and starting a number of innovative "virtual" public schools in states across the country.

The opportunities were exciting, but still the questions about life and how to live it rang in Gregg's head. His life was rich with his passions, from writing and sports to acoustic guitar gigs with musician friends at local bars, but the pieces of his life didn't fully cohere yet. He had thrown himself into his work with abandon, but it wasn't yet anchored by a unifying purpose. He wasn't in command of his life anymore.

The way to regain command, he realized, was to *take it back*. He could be in command simply by *deciding* to be. Life would not be something subject to the demands of a job or driven by others' priorities. Instead, it would be honored and savored.

It started with a simple choice. And it led to important realizations and big changes in his life. He married Kristina, his soul mate from Sweden whom he had dated long-distance for years; moved to Colorado to be near his family and the mountains; took a three-month sabbatical; went surfing in Mexico; scaled peaks in the Rockies with friends; embraced new life dreams for his growing family; started an entrepreneurial leadership development company with Christopher; and reawakened his passions for writing and for helping people lead good lives. Enter life entrepreneurship and this book.

As we wrote these pages, we kept asking: *How can we create extraordinary lives?* It was a question we sought to answer now.

The following pages capture what we have learned in the attempt. Our experiences have taught us that we feel most alive, happy, and sure of our direction when we are being true to ourselves, pursuing our purpose, and connecting and contributing to the people and world around us. And when things get off track, it helps to face reality and invoke renewal and reinvention to help get us back on *terra firma*. This approach is helping us lead better lives, and we are not alone.

Take Anita Sharpe. As a girl, she saw the Beatles perform on *The Ed Sullivan Show* and was transfixed. In that moment, she says, "Something just washed over me—that they are going to change the culture through the media. And it hit me that I wanted to do the same thing."

Anita went off to college in Tennessee and took a job as a writer for the award-winning *Atlanta Business Chronicle*. Brimming with ambition, she declared, "I think it would be fun to win a Pulitzer." The owner of the paper gently broke the news that such accolades typically go only to newspapers like the *New York Times* and *Wall Street Journal*. And so a personal goal was set. With the same tenacity and drive she demonstrated at the *Chronicle*, she earned a job as a reporter for the *Wall Street Journal*. By 1997, she was part of a team that won the famed prize for outstanding journalism.

To her surprise, she wasn't satisfied. "I had had a great run at the *Wall Street Journal*," she recalls. "It paid well for a journalist and had prestige. You think, 'Okay, this is it. I have reached the pinnacle of my career.' Everybody is patting you on the back. You feel like, 'I will be an idiot if I leave this.' But my gut said *No, this is not what I want to do*." She wanted "freedom to explore and learn, to pursue my own calling as opposed to being a card in somebody else's calling. . . . That old phrase—'It's not supposed to be fun, that's why they call it work'—that has always made my skin crawl. I just hate that. . . . Most people know in their heart and gut whether they are on the right path. If your brain has to get too involved in telling you, you're not on the right path."

So she took a leave to pursue her calling. At first, she cofounded a business-to-business online magazine called *dash30* with a former colleague from the *Journal*, Kevin Salwen. The magazine did well, but it wasn't "it" for her. It stopped being fun.

At the time, she read a book called *The Cultural Creatives,* which chronicled how fifty million people in the United States are prioritizing personal growth and focusing on making a contribution in the world instead of being driven solely by material gain.[4] For Anita, it was an awakening. It resonated with her values, and it also helped her spot an opportunity: there was no media outlet directly addressing this market segment.

With Kevin, she then launched a new business with the profits they earned from *dash30*. They created a national media company and magazine (originally called *Worthwhile* but renamed *Motto*) based on the notion that "it's impossible to have a meaningful life without meaningful work."[5]

For Anita, that's not just a theory. "What I am doing now," she says, "this is it. Everything is just coming together. Before, I was trying to play within the rules. Then I realized at some point, now I have to go out and do this myself. . . . My motto is that you create your own happiness. . . . To me, the biggest risk of all is an unlived life."

It is in this spirit that we offer this book.

So let's get started.

> *To be nobody-but-yourself—in a world which is*
> *doing its best, night and day, to make you everybody*
> *else—means to fight the hardest battle which any*
> *human being can fight; and never stop fighting.*
> —E. E. CUMMINGS

LIST OF INTERVIEWS

1. *Eric Adler.* Cofounder and managing director, SEED Foundation and Schools. Former dean of students at St. Paul's School in Baltimore. Former teacher and management consultant. Echoing Green Fellow.

2. *Karen Albrektsen.* Canadian retail executive turned restaurant entrepreneur. Founder and owner of Betty's Wok & Noodle Diner in Boston.

3. *Cory A. Booker.* Mayor of Newark, New Jersey. Recognized in numerous publications, including *U.S. News and World Report*, which named him one of "America's Best Leaders" in 2006.

4. *Stacey Boyd.* Founder and chief executive mom, Savvy Source for Parents. Founder and CEO, Global Learning Ventures; founder and former president and CEO, Project Achieve, Inc. Founding director and principal, Academy of the Pacific Rim Charter School.

5. *Warren Brown.* Founder, Cake Love. Former Department of Health and Human Services lawyer who founded his own community-based catering and cake company and now hosts a Food Network show called *Sugar Rush.* Voted one of *People* magazine's "Top 50 Eligible Bachelors."

6. *David Carmel.* Vice president, StemCyte, Inc., a leading stem cell therapeutics company. Cofounder of Jumpstart for Young Children and former White House fellow at the U.S. Department of the Treasury.

7. *Kevin Carroll.* Author, *Rules of the Red Rubber Ball.* Former executive, Nike. Founder, Katalyst Consultancy. Former head athletic trainer for the Philadelphia 76ers.

8. *Jack Chain.* Four-star general, U.S. Air Force (retired). Former fighter pilot, U.S. Air Force (two combat tours in Vietnam). Former commander, U.S. Strategic Air Command.

9. *Gerald Chertavian.* Founder and executive director, Year Up. Cofounder, Conduit Communications.

10. *Chip Conley.* Founder and CEO, Joie de Vivre Hotels. Author of several books, including *The Rebel Rules: Daring to Be Yourself in Business.*

11. *Mary Cutrufello.* Yale scholar turned rock star. Songwriter, singer, and guitar-playing virtuoso, with a unique blend of rock, blues, funk, and honky-tonk.

12. *Gun Denhart.* Founder, Hanna Andersson and Hanna Andersson Children's Foundation. Author, *Growing Local Value: How to Build Business Partnerships That Strengthen Your Community.*

13. *Robert Egger.* Founder and president, D.C. Central Kitchen. Author, *Begging for Change: The Dollars and Sense of Making Nonprofits Responsive, Efficient, and Rewarding for All.*

14. *Steve Ells.* Founder, chairman, and CEO, Chipotle.

15. *Gary Erickson.* Founder and owner, Clif Bar. Author, *Raising the Bar: Integrity and Passion in Life and Business: The Story of Clif Bar, Inc.*

16. *Mike Feinberg.* Cofounder, KIPP (Knowledge Is Power Program) Schools. Superintendent of KIPP Houston, former fifth-grade teacher with Teach for America in Houston.

17. *Michael Galgon.* Cofounder and chief strategy officer, aQuantive. Former demolition SCUBA diver with the U.S. Navy and AmeriCorps*VISTA volunteer.

18. *Bill George.* Professor of management practice, Harvard Business School. Author, *Authentic Leadership: Rediscovering the Secrets to Creating Lasting Value* and *True North: Discover Your Authentic Leadership.* Former chairman and CEO, Medtronic.

19. *Penny George.* President, George Family Foundation. Cofounder and past president, Bravewell Collaborative. Cancer survivor.

20. *Rob Glaser.* Founder and CEO, RealNetworks, Inc. Former vice president of multimedia and consumer systems, Microsoft.

21. *Seth Goldman.* Cofounder, president, and "TeaEO," Honest Tea. Former vice president, Calvert Social Investment Fund.

22. *Bridget Bradley Gray.* Founder, Wiggle Room. Former executive, D.C. Public Charter School Board.

23. *David Gray.* Associate pastor, Georgetown Presbyterian Church. Director, Workforce and Family Program, New America

Foundation. Former acting assistant secretary for policy, U.S. Department of Labor. Author, *Faith in Service.*

24. *John Hickenlooper.* Mayor of Denver, Colorado. Founder, Wynkoop Brewing Company.

25. *John Horan-Kates.* Founder and president, Vail Leadership Institute. Former president, East West Marketing. Former vice president of marketing, Vail Resorts. Founder and former president, Vail Valley Foundation.

26. *Max Israel.* Founder and CEO, Customerville. Founder and chairman, Play & Music Franchise Systems. Founder and former CEO, Bridgehouse Foods International. Competitive Ironman triathlete.

27. *Jael Kampfe.* Manager, Lazy E-L Ranch. Founder, Four Times Foundation. Former professional dancer.

28. *Emmet B. Keeffe III.* Cofounder and CEO, iRise.

29. *Peter Kellner.* Cofounder and managing director, Richmond Management LLC. Founder, Camp Kellner Media, LLC. Cofounder, Endeavor Global. Fulbright scholar.

30. *Natalie Killassy.* Founder and managing director, Stitch Wise, South Africa. Selected as an Endeavor entrepreneur in 2004.

31. *Suzanne Klahr.* Founder, Build.org. Ashoka fellow. Honored with the Social Visionary 2000 Award and the Entrepreneurial Spirit Award for Entrepreneurial Teaching by the National Foundation for Teaching Entrepreneurship. Faculty adjunct at Stanford Law School.

32. *Randy Komisar.* Partner, Kleiner Perkins Caufield & Byers. Cofounder, Claris Corporation. Former CEO, LucasArts Entertainment and Crystal Dynamics. Consulting professor of entrepreneurship at Stanford University. Author, *The Monk and the Riddle.*

33. *Richard Leider.* Founding principal, Inventure Group. Author, *The Power of Purpose.*

34. *Larry Leith.* Founder, Tokyo Joe's, a restaurant chain in Denver.

35. *David Levin.* Cofounder, KIPP (Knowledge Is Power Program) Schools; superintendent of the KIPP Academy in the South Bronx, New York. Former fifth-grade teacher with Teach for America in Houston.

36. *Paul Lightfoot.* President and CEO, AL Systems. Founder and CEO, Foodline. Triathlete.

37. *Linda Mason.* Chairman and cofounder, Bright Horizons Family Solutions. Author, *The Working Mother's Guide to Life: Strategies, Secrets, and Solutions.* Cofounder, Horizons for Homeless Children. Managed large-scale relief operations overseas. Received *Working Mother* magazine designation as one of the "25 Most Influential Mothers in America."

38. *Simi Mir.* Partner, Katona & Mir. Producing and directing documentary on Kashmiri Hindus and Muslims.

39. *Paul Nasrani.* Founder, Adirondack Creamery. Partner and treasurer, Firesafe Corporation. Treasurer, Atlantic Bag Company. Former CFO, Strategic Workforce Solutions.

40. *Will Pearson.* Founder and "El Presidente," *mental_floss.*

41. *Jared Polis.* Founder, Blue_Mountain_Arts.com. Founder, ProFlowers.com.

42. *Steve Quisenberry.* Founder and CEO, 105 Meridian. Owner, Mountainsmith, Inc. Former Colorado Entrepreneur of the Year.

43. *Inez Russell.* Founder and Executive Director, Friends for Life.

44. *Howard Schultz.* Chairman and chief global strategist, Starbucks. Coauthor, *Pour Your Heart into It.* Former owner, Seattle Supersonics.

45. *Buie Seawell.* Chair, Business Ethics and Legal Studies, University of Denver. Civil rights activist, minister, theologian, attorney, environmental activist, political leader, professor. Former candidate for U.S. Senate from Colorado. Former chairman, Colorado Democratic Party.

46. *Anita Sharpe.* Cofounding editor, MOTTO. Editor in chief, *Atlanta Business Chronicle.* Pulitzer Prize-winning writer, *Wall Street Journal.*

47. *Murem Sharpe.* Founder and CEO, Evoca LLC. Former executive, Pitney Bowes.

48. *Billy Shore.* Founder and executive director, Share Our Strength. Chairman, Community Wealth Ventures, Inc. Author of *Revolutions of the Heart, The Cathedral Within,* and *The Light of Conscience.*

49. *Kim Smith.* Cofounder, senior advisor, and former CEO, NewSchools Venture Fund, venture philanthropy firm in Silicon Valley. Founding team member, Teach for America. Faculty adjunct at Stanford University.

LIFE ENTREPRENEURS

PART ONE

SURVEYING THE LANDSCAPE

CHAPTER ONE

UNDERSTANDING LIFE ENTREPRENEURSHIP

I would rather be a superb meteor, every atom of me in magnificent glow, than a sleepy and permanent planet. The proper function of man is to live, not to exist.
—JACK LONDON

Some people don't just live; they *lead* a life. They don't sit around waiting for a lucky break; they create opportunities for themselves. They go after their dreams and bring them to life. Rather than bending to the status quo, they change it. Rather than being imprisoned by circumstance, they turn it to their advantage.

They assess their direction in life and determine whether it fits with who they are and what they want. They develop a vision of the good life, devise a plan for how to attain it, go for it, and check their progress along the way—all the while addressing, with creativity and flexibility, the inevitable obstacles that arise. As with any great effort, their work is never done but ever-evolving, and it is often inspiring to those around them.

Welcome to the territory of *life entrepreneurs.*

The word *entrepreneur* comes from the French word *entre-prendre,* "to undertake." The entrepreneur, then, is the acting person who recognizes an opportunity and then, compelled by an idea of how reality can be improved, takes action to produce a more valuable outcome. In the process, she assumes the attendant risks and reaps the rewards through ownership. By applying creativity to a particular challenge or opportunity, entrepreneurs alter reality and expand our sense of what is possible.

In business literature, entrepreneurship is often broken into four defining components: creation, commitment, risk, and ownership. Entrepreneurs are also commonly thought of as being visionary, driven, innovative, intuitive, self-directed, confident, opportunistic, resourceful, and persistent.

THE LIFE ENTREPRENEUR

That leads us to the *life entrepreneur*—one who creates a life of significance through opportunity recognition, innovation, and action. Rather than being driven by the opportunity to create an innovative enterprise, a life entrepreneur is driven by the chance to create a life of significance.

In many ways, life entrepreneurs use the same tools that a business or social entrepreneur uses to build a new enterprise, creatively applying the best of those start-up practices toward building a better life. But being a life entrepreneur is about developing an authentic, personal vision for our *life* and then going after it. It's about awakening to the opportunities around us and setting audacious goals. It's about building healthy support systems and marshaling resources. It's about taking action and making a difference. And it's about taking time out for reflection so we can renew ourselves for the road ahead.

A man from Boston once embodied this spirit. He had a difficult childhood, didn't attend much formal school, and ran away. As a young man, he worked hard and borrowed money to set himself up in the printing business. Then he became a father, ran a bookstore, earned enough money to buy and run a newspaper, wrote thought-provoking columns, dabbled in political cartoons, organized civic groups, published books, held elected office, served as an ambassador, helped launch environmental cleanup projects, and created a library, hospital, fire company, and insurance program.

He also verified the nature of electricity through an experiment with kites, helped to draft the Declaration of Independence, and signed the U.S. Constitution. His name, as you may have surmised, is Benjamin Franklin.

Most people know him as an American "founding father," but he was also a classic life entrepreneur. His whole life comprised launching new enterprises in service of his community and country while also committing himself to self-improvement, discovery, reflection, and renewal. He is the one, after all, who admonished us: "God helps them that help themselves." And "Drive thy Business, let not that drive thee." And observed that "The noblest question in the world is, *What Good may I do in it?*"

Few of us approach our potential as fully and vigorously as Ben Franklin. There's a big dividing line between ordinary lives and extraordinary ones, and many of us pass our time well short of that line. But one of time's jealously guarded secrets is that the line is imaginary. It exists only in our heads. There is, it turns out, no limit to the number of extraordinary lives that can be realized, no quota on good lives to be claimed. Yet too many of us cling fiercely to imaginary limits we have set for ourselves or accepted from others.

In the pages ahead, we will learn from fifty-five different people from a wide array of backgrounds who have shed their imaginary limits. These are the stories of ordinary people who have had the imagination, courage, and resolve to integrate and enrich their lives in ways that are both extraordinary and instructive. We have much to learn from them, starting with how we can make our lives entrepreneurial in service of our dreams.

AN INTEGRATED LIFE

In college, Stacey Boyd discovered a passion for education reform. Writing her senior thesis on different ways to design and run effective schools and school systems, she became enthralled by the Japanese system of education. So she moved to Japan, taught middle school for a year, and immersed herself in the Japanese learning culture. She returned to the United States to work for a start-up company called the Edison Project that led a massive effort to redesign public schools to make them more effective.

In business school, she had what she calls a "lightning bolt" idea of starting a school based on what she had learned. She had always thought it would be twenty years before she started her own school, but one day she wondered, *What am I waiting for?*

At age twenty-six and just two weeks after graduating, Stacey founded the Academy of the Pacific Rim, a charter public school dedicated to providing inner-city Boston students with a world-class education that married the best of the East—high standards, discipline, and character education—with the best of the West—individualism, creativity, and diversity.

As "PacRim" developed a sterling reputation nationally, Stacey was confronted with a major challenge: too much was happening inside the school that she, as principal, couldn't keep track of. She envisioned a technology system that would help principals, teachers, and parents all do their job better through systematic sharing of information about how students were doing.

Late at night after long days at school, she found herself developing a technology platform to do just that. Once finished, it became a tremendous asset to the school staff and parents. Word got around, and people started visiting the academy from far and wide to observe the technology in action. Soon she was invited to speak at conferences, and foundations approached her about deploying the system in other schools. She knew she was on to something. And so Project Achieve was born, a start-up company whose comprehensive information management system was eventually made available to 15 percent of U.S. public schools through a partnership with the U.S. Department of Education.

In the meantime, Stacey had fallen in love with a fellow education reformer named Scott Hamilton, and they settled in San Francisco. During a trip together in Botswana, Stacey started thinking "how exciting it would be if we were able to take what we had done in the U.S. and apply that to the developing world." So she started Global Learning Ventures, an education technology consultancy, and found herself jetting across the globe, working day and night.

When she became pregnant, she was forced to reevaluate. The entrepreneurial path she was on didn't leave much time for other pursuits, much less raising a family. "It was really Gracie's birth that made me take a step back," she recalls, "because the last thing I wanted to do was board a plane to Libya. I was a lot more excited about wandering up the steps to the nursery."

Her priorities changed yet again when Scott was struck by a car while riding his motor scooter in San Francisco. His skull fractured as the helmet cracked open. At first, the doctors didn't know if he would make it. Then, they didn't know if he would regain consciousness, proper brain functioning, or his memory. Eventually, he astonished everyone by making a full recovery. Through that harrowing ordeal, Scott and Stacey gained new perspective and urgency about their life together.

Settling back into family life, Stacey began searching for preschools for Gracie. She was surprised to learn that there was no independent consumer rating service to help parents navigate the maze of choices. Recognizing a very personal need and feeling her entrepreneurial instincts kick back into gear, she seized the moment and launched the Savvy Source for Parents, an information hub and network for parents looking for quality educational options.

As she launched the company, she was cognizant of the fact that her previous start-ups had been all-consuming. This time, she was committed to having an integrated life and a job with a reasonable and flexible schedule. Wrestling with that dilemma, she had a breakthrough. Stacey built a virtual company comprising one hundred part-time working moms across the country, with all employees and contractors working from home. Together, they created a family-friendly company that produces a web-based guide to nearly all the preschools in the United States. It is now expanding into providing consumer ratings for camps, classes, educational books and toys, learning activities, and more.

She recounts, "I feel like I have found a way to lead a really entrepreneurial company that is growing in leaps and bounds, but also to be a good mom and be with Gracie more or less every waking hour. . . . At Savvy, we all have young children and they are our number one priority. Work is important but not the preeminent part of our lives. Running this organization is radically different. I would say 95 percent of our work is done in the morning before the kids wake up, in the afternoon when they take naps, and at night when they go to bed. I'm telling you, everything gets done faster and better. It's extraordinary. . . ."

Last year, Stacey and Scott decided to move to Jackson Hole, Wyoming, a place where they had always imagined retiring. Their rationale was simple: *Why wait?* After Scott's accident, she started asking herself: "Am I doing things that allow me to live the way

I want, serve the way I want, and be the parent I want to be? The last thing we wanted to do was live in a way that was talking about tomorrow instead of living it today."

ANSWERING A CALL

Like Stacey, David Gray has also struggled with adversity and competing demands. His achievement in life has sometimes been a mixed blessing. Through each life chapter, he has succeeded through a combination of talent, hard work, and meticulous preparation—from national speech championships in high school, to on-campus leadership at Yale, to the marketing fast track at Procter & Gamble, a dual master's degree, and senior policy roles in the U.S. Senate and U.S. Department of Labor. Through it all, he maintained his easygoing nature, sense of humor, and uncanny ability to connect with people.

Long ago, he "rejected the notion of having one career for your entire life." That freed him up to explore a variety of paths, but it also led to what he calls a "tortured process" of decision making about his next career moves. Sometimes he got stuck, feeling overwhelmed by a parade of options—having so many interests that it was hard to choose one and forgo the others. And with success came inertia. The catch-22 was that the more successful he was, the harder it would be to start over and try something new.

Meanwhile, something was missing in his life. While he was in college, his younger sister had died in a tragic car accident in Britain. By going through that suffering, he found what he calls "a maturity that comes from loss." It moved him to tap more deeply into his spiritual core. He was powerfully affected by the ministry he received as he grieved, not only from family and friends but also from clergy. He says, "You talk to anyone who's suffered some blow to the stomach and you learn more from your challenges than you do from your successes. It helps you relate to the fullness of life, with all its ups and downs." Finding strength and stability in faith, he decided to enter divinity school. He continued in various high-ranking government jobs as he pursued ministry and volunteered in the local hospital.

Then one day he was offered a significant policy position at the White House. To many, the decision to accept would be a no-brainer, but David wasn't so sure. With that job, he knew he would rarely see his new wife, Bridget, and he would have to put off his ordination as a minister. He was also looking for some downtime after an intense two years of working hard while taking classes at night and writing a book. "I wanted to detox from my work in government," he says. "My identity was wrapped up in government, with an unhealthy amount of focus." But the allure of the job offer was not lost on him. After a few long days of wrestling with the decision and consulting with his family and friends, he respectfully declined the White House offer.

It was a shock to many. How could he walk away from such a prestigious job?

The decision was difficult, but in the end his rationale was clear and firm: he was committed to the path he was on—prioritizing his marriage, starting a family, finishing his divinity studies, and becoming ordained—answering a call that he could no longer ignore. "The things that I'm most proud of," he recalls, "have to do with touching people's lives at particular times, many of them very difficult times in their lives."

Today, Reverend Gray is working as a minister in a variety of contexts, including a church and college campus. He's even bringing that perspective to his work at a think tank in its "Healthy Families Initiative." Instead of approaching ministry as a "political guy," he is approaching his life and work from the perspective of his values of faith, family, and service.

Time will tell how he pieces it all together, but there is no doubt that he has crossed a threshold. When faced with one of his life's biggest decisions yet, he stopped and listened to his heart.

PUTTING *LIFE* BACK INTO OUR LIVES

These days there are many people who, like Stacey and David, are rethinking what they want from life, seizing control of the tiller, and becoming captains of their fate. In his book, *Free Agent Nation*, Daniel Pink points out that, counting temporary workers, microbusinesses, and freelancers or "soloists," there are over

thirty-three million free agents in the U.S. workforce today—
more than 25 percent of the total. Every year, seventeen million
Americans change their jobs. These trends are now going global.
Pink describes the dream of today's young people: "Not to climb
through an organization, or even to accept a job at one, but to
create their own gig on their own terms."[1]

What is going on here? Either we have a serious case of
professional attention deficit disorder or we are not finding
what we are looking for in the usual places. Of course, many of
these employment changes are externally imposed. The pressures of a competitive global economy rife with outsourcing have
led to widespread layoffs and diminished job security in many
industries. So these trends are being driven externally by economic and social forces as well as internally by individual motivations and choices.

Today, there is a burgeoning interest in forging a new path
in life that includes rewarding work that is also consistent with
one's values. Here we arrive at a dilemma. On the one hand,
people are looking for opportunity, challenge, and the chance
to develop their talents, achieve success, and have an impact. On
the other hand, they are looking for a happy home life, rewarding friendships, active lifestyle, close-knit community, and time to
pursue other interests. In the meantime, we are being squeezed
with practical obligations and financial pressures that sometimes
present us with stark choices and painful trade-offs.

It is the life entrepreneur who is able to thread the needle,
preserving quality of life while thriving in his chosen context.
And it is the forward-thinking organization that attracts and
retains talented workers by creating dynamic and intrapreneurial[2]
opportunities that can flex with the priorities and schedules of
today's go-getters while maintaining (or even increasing) productivity. As Jeanie Duck of the Boston Consulting Group says, "It's a
myth that companies are filled with highly capable people that
are willing to work 24/7. It's not true. The companies that crack
this will have their pick of talented people."[3] Today, we see more
and more examples of organizations addressing these trends,
including the Business Talent Group in Los Angeles and Mind
Farm in Washington, D.C. We detect an urgency to all of this, but

it is fair to assume that the world is not going to decelerate as we figure it all out.

YOUR OWN "SECRET OFFICE"

Max Israel is someone who is addressing this issue for both himself and others. In college he launched an export company that did business in developing countries. For ten years he traveled to every corner of the globe and grew the company. Back home in Seattle, Washington, his family was also growing. After a while the trade-off was becoming clear: run a great company taking him to faraway places or be a great husband and father. The competing demands were too much at odds.

With child number three on the way, he and his wife decided to change direction and acquire and run a collection of local child-care franchises together. A new world opened up, giving Max the space to reconnect with his family, community, and passions. These changes inspired him to set a personal goal:

"Each year, I try to take twenty-five workweek days and spend them hiking, biking, or on the water someplace. It's like having your own secret office with the world's best views. These aren't bank holidays or the days between Christmas and New Year's. They're midweek days right in the heart of the year when everyone else is at their desk. My best creative thinking is on these days. The places I go are inspiring, and exercise tends to calm my mind and help me see the big picture. Following these days, I try to resist the urge to catch up on e-mails at night. Instead I'll write or think about what occupied my mind that day."

In that "secret office," Max hatched a plan to expand nationally with a software system he had built for his franchises. With that, he sees an opportunity to help others lead an integrated life as well. As we write, he is establishing a network of dynamic salespeople who want to develop and own their sales territory while maintaining balance in their lives. Max relates, "We want people who will value their investment in us not only because it makes money, but because it allows them to lead fuller lives." He believes those people will do a better job over the long haul and that they can build something of great value together—a true win-win.

PATTERNS OF LIVING

Part of what makes Max a life entrepreneur is that he has ample amounts of both drive and direction. In many ways, how we approach drive and direction in our lives determines whether we lead a life of limits or one of unfettered fulfillment. As we will see, strength in one does not compensate for weakness in another. They must work in concert. Life entrepreneurship is a lifelong process of deploying both drive and direction to create an extraordinary life.

DRIVE

Drive is the motivation or desire to go for it. Those of us with drive have a passion to commit ourselves to something—often something much bigger than ourselves. This breathes life into everything we do and fuels our motivation to take risks and act.

Karen Albrektsen had her drive tested in her early thirties. After a rocky breakup with her husband in Toronto, she was in search of a fresh start. She had always dreamed of starting her own restaurant. Against the advice of her family and friends, she packed up a U-Haul truck and aimed her life in a new direction: cooking school in Chicago. As the Sears Tower came into view, she "saw the page close on a chapter, with a whole new wide chapter ahead of me."

Her plan was to study at a top culinary school while immersing herself in the restaurant trade as a waitress. It all made sense on paper, but after three months she squared off against self-doubt: *What have I done?* She was far from home, alone, and working crazy hours, slogging through long days in school followed by nights in the restaurant working for next to nothing. With no time to make friends, loneliness set in. This was her big test. Though tempted to pack it up and head back north, she summoned the drive to stay the course and persist in her new life direction.

"Those were dark days," Karen remembers. "To get by, I focused on why I was there and the end goal." She also searched mightily for people to support her dream. She hit the jackpot when she cold-called a respected restaurant consultant in Boston who agreed to help her, and then again in finding a dynamic new business partner who shared her passion and embraced the vision of creating a funky new Asian-fusion restaurant. In 1999, her persistent drive paid off: she moved to Boston and opened Betty's Wok & Noodle Diner across the street from Symphony Hall. It has since become a mainstay for hungry students and young professionals flocking to its healthy dishes and cocktail concoctions (especially the sake martinis and mojitos).

Karen has reinvented her life, moving from heartbreak to new adventures and relationships and, with it, gaining newfound confidence. With her inner drive firing, she is now turning her attention toward new entrepreneurial directions.

DIRECTION

Direction is drive's companion, the harnessing force that channels our drive toward a desired destination. Our direction comes from our core identity and gives us a sense of where we should be heading. Those with a strong sense of direction in life are able to develop an aspirational vision for what their future can hold. When new opportunities arise, they can assess them in the context of that direction.

For Randy Komisar, direction is more of a wide swath on the horizon to head toward than a specific port. Once CEO of LucasArts Entertainment, he reinvented himself as a "virtual CEO" serving a number of start-ups in Silicon Valley and then again as a partner at renowned venture capital firm Kleiner Perkins Caufield & Byers. Though he has changed careers several times, "My life is not adrift," he explains. "There is no road map, but there is a horizon that I'm moving towards. That horizon is broad, but it is informed by what I believe. . . . The keel to your boat needs to be your values, your principles, your beliefs, and some sense of purpose, but that needs to be aimed at a horizon, not a point of latitude and longitude, because that point may turn out to be irrelevant."

Four Patterns of Living

These elements—drive and direction—reveal four common patterns of living that most of us fall into. It turns out that we can assess our drive and direction to help gauge our current life circumstance. In so doing, we can identify what elements are missing and then go do something about it. At any point in our lives, we are likely to be in one of four possible life patterns: we can be low in both direction and drive (what we call *drifters*); high in direction but low in drive (*passengers*); high in drive but low in direction (*seekers*); or high in both drive and direction (*captains*) (see Figure 1.1).

Note: To take an assessment and plot yourself on this matrix, please go to www.lifeentrepreneurs.com.

In this section we address each of these four patterns with a brief vignette showing how it plays out in dynamic fashion.

Drifters

Drifters are on a raft letting the wind and waves take them out to sea. They go with the flow, without a sense of where they are

FIGURE 1.1. Patterns of Living.

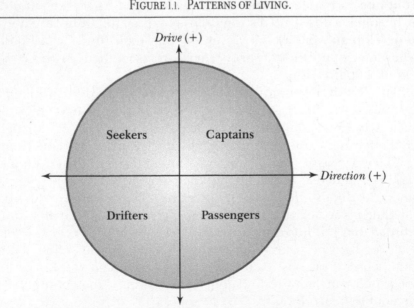

going or the drive to figure it out. With luck, their voyage can lead to interesting adventures and learning experiences that they can draw on later.

Mary Cutrufello is a Yale graduate turned rock star. She is a dynamic and explosive singer, songwriter, and guitar-playing virtuoso, with a unique blend of rock, blues, funk, and honky-tonk. In the course of her notable musical career, she released several albums and toured the world, but was suddenly stricken with a case of infected lymph nodes in her neck that caused her to lose her voice. Banished from her dream world of music, she started to drift in life, adjusting to her new reality and yearning to recapture her drive and direction.

Says Cutrufello, "I'm sort of in that castaway mode right now. Things happen. It's not anybody's fault. But it shouldn't change who you are or how you approach what you're doing. . . . I'm working towards getting back onto my path. The things that happen, they don't define you unless you let them." Since we spoke, her voice has healed and her drive and direction have come roaring back; she has just completed a new album and is starting to tour again. But during that healing time, her travails caused her to go deeper and get acquainted with who she is when she wasn't at one with her Fender Telecaster guitar.

Passengers

Passengers know where they want to go in life but haven't yet summoned, or have somehow lost, the drive to get there. Passengers often lose their drive through circumstance—such as an illness, death of a loved one, or professional crisis. Sometimes they lose it through compromise, such as the common rationalization that they will chase their dreams later—or that it is better to take an existing trail than blaze a new one.

In their twenties, Beth and Devon Santa were both making a living at office jobs that paid well but left them flat. After they met and fell in love, everything changed. They discovered they had a common passion (friends call it an obsession) for sailing and adventure, coupled with an independent spirit. So they sold off most of their worldly goods and struck out on a seafaring adventure: starting a business that moved sailboats from port to port for races and regattas, allowing them to be out on the sea for much of the year. They have since expanded the business to include other services at local marinas and have started a family. Today, they are still madly in love, happy to have ocean waves beneath their floating office, and grateful to have reignited the drive behind their shared direction.

Seekers

Seekers have drive but haven't yet discovered the horizon they want to sail toward. They have an itch to see new lands and find themselves wandering. They are yearning for direction, not yet sure where they want to end up.

Growing up in southern California, Chip Conley had no shortage of drive. As a boy, he started a restaurant in his parents' dining room, launched a neighborhood newspaper, and even organized an "annual Olympics" for the kids on his street. "I was the one who was going to be president by the time I was thirty-five," he muses. In college, he was a star athlete. He got into the real estate business through his Uncle Bruce, a maverick developer. He recalls, "I was surrounded mostly by guys who were complete testosterone junkies. It was a 'good old boy' network." It was a "habitat," as he calls it, where he didn't feel at home.

By his senior year in college, Chip had started a real estate consulting firm with a fraternity brother but soon decided that it wasn't for him. He was seeking. He enrolled in business school right after college and interned at Morgan Stanley in New York City. "Here I was in New York," he recalls. "I was twenty-two, wearing suspenders, smoking cigars, hanging out with the guys, doing deals. And I was coming out as a gay man."

Chip recounts, "I was dying inside. I was so possessed by trying to make you love me for my achievements that I was actually creating this identity that was disconnected from myself. I wanted people to love me for the hologram I created of myself. . . . When I told my dad I was gay, it really wiped the slate clean in terms of what I wanted to do."

Starting over, he found his direction. On his twenty-sixth birthday, he finished writing a business plan for an avant-garde hotel based on a spirited rock 'n' roll theme. It was a transformative moment. "Within two months," he says, "I not only found the property but bought it with investors' money and was off to the races."

Today, this onetime seeker is the largest boutique hotel operator in California. All thirty of his hotels have creative designs and motifs. He says, "I actually called the company 'Joie de Vivre' for myself first and foremost—it was a reminder to me that this is why I am doing this. Today, I've created a habitat where I can actually dare to be myself." He also wrote a book called *The Rebel Rules: Daring to Be Yourself in Business*. For Chip, becoming himself meant channeling his strong drive into a direction that was aligned with who he was becoming.

Captains

Captains know where they want to go in life and have the drive to get there, actively steering in that direction. They assume command of their lives, perhaps out of instinct or conviction, taking the helm of their ships and steering purposefully toward a horizon that intrigues them.

Take Kevin Johnson. During his twelve-year National Basketball Association career, "KJ" was a three-time NBA All-Star and one of only four players to average at least twenty points and ten assists per game over three seasons. Since retiring from basketball, he has focused his legendary drive in a new direction. That includes founding and working with a number of community organizations in his native hometown of Sacramento, California: the St. Hope community revitalization project, St. Hope Public Schools (a public charter school district serving two thousand students), St. Hope Neighborhood Corps (training young people to be community leaders), St. Hope Development Company (a real estate company that has developed an estimated $15 million worth of projects in the community), and an art gallery. His focus is on bringing lasting hope to his hometown, particularly through quality education. From captain of his team to captain of these community service efforts, Kevin embodies the better qualities of life entrepreneurship.[4]

This picture of drifters, passengers, seekers, and captains is not static. These are general patterns that we move in and out of over time. And of course our lives are not one-dimensional: different parts of our lives may contain higher drive or direction than others. A young professional in Tokyo's financial district may be directed professionally but less so in her personal or romantic life.

The point is not to resign ourselves to one of these quadrants or berate ourselves for not being a captain all the time but rather to use these tools as a catalyst for change. We should also recognize that there are seasons in life—times to drift a little and enjoy the ride, times to seek deeper meaning and greater self-awareness through purposeful reflection. Without those periods in our life, we sacrifice a bit of our humanity. Life's winds can change unexpectedly, requiring us to navigate in and out of these quadrants through reflection, renewal, and reinvention.

The good news for those of us not satisfied with our lives is that we can change where we stand. Movement along new avenues is always possible, but much is required of those who seek to change. The question quickly arises: Change toward what? That is, what are we aiming toward? That's no small question. As we begin to address it and seek a proper repository for our aspirations, we start to catch glimpses of "the good life."

CREATING THE GOOD LIFE

What then shall I do this morning? How we spend
our days is, of course, how we spend our lives. . . .
There is no shortage of good days. It is good lives
that are hard to come by.
—ANNIE DILLARD

Life entrepreneurship can help us realize what Aristotle called "the good life." He believed that in the good life we find happiness—not in the contemporary sense of a pleasurable (and often fleeting) feeling of contentment, but in the ancient sense of *eudaimonia*, meaning happiness through virtuous action, habits of moral excellence, and a full flourishing of self. The good life is achieved by putting into practice what we believe, fulfilling our very nature, and attaining excellence as people and citizens—the very best of us.[5]

Creating the good life is about pursuing our potential in a deliberate and purposeful way. According to psychologist Carl Rogers, "The good life is a process, not a state of being. It is a direction, not a destination." For increasing numbers of people, an entrepreneurial life is a promising path to the good life.

Of course, not everyone will choose it, but it is an increasingly attractive choice, especially among rising generations. And it doesn't have to be a complicated endeavor.

Authors Richard Leider and David Shapiro define the good life simply as "living in the place you belong, with the people you love, doing the right work, on purpose. . . . Designing the good life becomes, then, 'a simple matter' of finding and keeping adequate space for love, place, and work in your life. In other words, reaching for and holding on to what really matters in your life and letting go of the responsibilities and commitments that do not."[6]

Still, creating the good life entails substantial risk. It can mean starting over and relinquishing degrees of financial and emotional security. It can mean shedding layers of a safe, stable, and predictable existence. It can mean the possibility of failure by conventional measures. It can mean disappointing people who expect us to continue along the same road. It is much easier to walk along prescribed paths than to blaze our own trail. But how much do we forgo when we retreat to safety and conformity?

A hunger for the good life lies deep within us all. But it requires an honest evaluation of who we are and how we are living. Some manage to avoid these hard questions for years, or even for a whole lifetime—diligently going with each year's flow without pausing to imagine other possible destinations. With the passing of years, our childhood dreams are pierced by reality. Our daily lives are filled with obligations and pressures. As we grow older, we drift away from "what could be" toward a life shaped not by personal vision or calling but by circumstance and compromise.

But occasionally we catch glimpses of what the future could hold in store—our own personal vision of the good life—and an inner restlessness is rekindled. That restlessness needs an outlet for all its stored energy. It needs a path for channeling it in a worthy direction.

THE PATH OF THE LIFE ENTREPRENEUR

The path of the life entrepreneur is just such a thing. Here we introduce that path, first by describing its specific features, then by addressing how we should prepare ourselves to walk it, and finally by outlining the major steps to take along the way.

EXHIBIT 1.1.   THE WINDING PATH.

THE PATH IS WINDING

The pages ahead offer a logical framework for taking big life ideas and putting them into action. We want to emphasize at the outset, though, that the life entrepreneur's path is decidedly nonlinear (see Exhibit 1.1). This winding path can cut back on itself, jump ahead, and zigzag unexpectedly. After all, this is life we are talking about. The steps on the path may look simple and straightforward on paper, but in reality they are far from it. Sometimes, they flow sequentially, but that is the exception. Often they double back, take us on scouting expeditions up new trails, or confront us all at once and threaten to overwhelm us. For some, the path makes sense only on looking back. The bottom line is that life entrepreneurship does have a natural framework to follow, but it frequently requires improvisational choreography of order and disorder, resulting in a dance that is sometimes chaotic and always unique.

Each person's path to becoming a life entrepreneur is different. Some are meticulous in their planning before embarking; others leap right into it. Some are like chess players, thinking several moves ahead; others are like abstract artists, finding meaning and richness through a more spontaneous and playful process.

How to Walk the Path

A follow-on point about the (winding) path of the life entrepreneur is that walking the path is only half the battle. *How* we walk the path is just as important. The mind-sets we adopt, approaches we take, and provisions we stuff into our rucksacks for the journey ahead are just as important as the steps themselves. It is this combination of the path and how we walk it that determines the quality and character of our lives.

Based on our research and observations, life entrepreneurs are best served when they summon and employ the following on their journey:

- *Authentic Integrity:* integration of all aspects of our lives in a way that coheres with our true nature, flowing from our core identity (purpose and values)
- *Deep Awareness:* being alert to who we are and the changing needs, challenges, and opportunities that surround us
- *Breakthrough Innovation:* game-changing, applied creativity that helps us transcend the boundaries of the present
- *Courage to Try:* an openness to act in spite of our fears and a predisposition toward going for it
- *Purposeful Spontaneity:* a willingness to let go, improvise, and seize new opportunities in a way that resonates with our deepest essence and reason for being
- *Adaptive Persistence:* tailoring our approach to the circumstances while persevering through adversity
- *Pervasive Service:* an ethic of contribution as a defining feature of our lives

Each of these themes will be drawn out in the chapters ahead. Each one is necessary. We may be able to hike for miles without one or another, but over the span of time we will need all of them.

THE STEPS ON THE PATH

Here we arrive at the trailhead. There are several common steps on the path of the life entrepreneur that, when taken in conjunction with one another, greatly increase the chances of success and, ultimately, a life of significance. Not coincidentally, each of these steps headlines the ensuing chapters. Here is a preview:

The Path of the Life Entrepreneur
1. Discovering Core Identity
2. Awakening to Opportunity
3. Envisioning the Future
4. Developing Goals and Strategies
5. Building Healthy Support Systems
6. Taking Action and Making a Difference
7. Embracing Renewal and Reinvention

1. Discovering Core Identity
This is our compass. At its heart are our values and purpose. These are informed by external factors such as our personal history, current circumstances, and relationships as well as internal factors such as our needs, strengths, and passions. Establishing an authentic orientation (a "true north") is a lifelong project. Without a strong core identity, the steps that follow are likely to lead us astray.

2. Awakening to Opportunity
With deep self-awareness, we become more aware of opportunities around us that resonate with our core identity. This includes being "switched on" to the world around us, being able to assess opportunities as they arise, and figuring out how to translate these promising ideas into attractive and actionable opportunities.

3. Envisioning the Future
The notion of vision is commonly applied to an organization, but it can also be applied to our lives: What do we envision for who

we will be and what we will do with our lives? This is best imagined in long increments, such as a decade or even an entire lifetime. Our vision is unearthed from within even as it is informed by opportunity and circumstance, reflecting a nexus of internal and external elements. With vivid clarity, our vision should raise our sights, inspiring us to something audacious and worthy of pursuit.

4. Developing Goals and Strategies

Successful entrepreneurs will tell you that without a well-informed game plan an enterprise is likely to fall flat. The same can be true in life. Developing goals and strategies provides needed clarity and focus. Goals should be purposeful and prioritized, clear and measurable, and challenging but achievable. Once our goals are established, we can identify the gaps between our current reality and envisioned future and start planning to fill those gaps by leveraging existing resources and attracting new ones.

5. Building Healthy Support Systems

None of us can create a life of significance on our own. Having a robust support system infused with healthy, diverse relationships helps us achieve our life goals. It can also provide shelter from the inevitable storms that roll in. If we are doing right by others, this web of support can create what we call a *positive network effect*, enhancing our ability to make a difference in the world.

6. Taking Action and Making a Difference

The preceding steps are academic unless we assume risks and take action. The essential elements of taking action are having the courage to try, leaping through windows of opportunity, entering the arena, creatively finding ways to serve, adapting and persisting, and erasing limits. What's more, we must avoid the common pitfalls that trap many entrepreneurs and recognize the cost of *not* taking action.

7. Embracing Renewal and Reinvention

Sometimes renewal is necessary. At times we must step back and take a look around, assessing where we have come from and where we are going. It is vital to find regular times to reconnect with our core identity and prepare to initiate a new set of adventures. We must be careful not to push ourselves back into "superhero" action mode before we are replenished and ready. And when renewal is insufficient, we turn to reinvention—making wholesale changes in the fabric of our lives, stitching them together with new material better suited to the days ahead.

This framework of core identity, opportunity recognition, vision, goals and strategy, support systems, action, and renewal has worked for countless business and social entrepreneurs across generations. In this book we show how it can also be a powerful model for approaching our lives. We address each of these steps in a subsequent chapter. Before doing so, we first tell the stories of three life entrepreneurs in action. In their stories, we will see how life entrepreneurship has played out in the full arc of their lives, how they coped with difficult decisions and personal setbacks, how they prioritized their actions and behaviors, and how the entrepreneurial path helped them, ultimately, to create extraordinary lives.

CHAPTER TWO

LIFE ENTREPRENEURS IN ACTION

If you ask me what I have come to do in this world . . .
I will reply: I'm here to live my life out loud.
—EMILE ZOLA

Raised in a middle-class New Jersey neighborhood by parents who were civil-rights activists and among the first African-American executives at IBM, Cory Booker was taught the value of service early in life. At Stanford University he volunteered as a youth outreach coordinator in East Palo Alto and worked at a suicide hotline. He was also a standout tight end on the football team and was approached by professional scouts from the National Football League.

After an outstanding performance against Notre Dame's famous "Fighting Irish" squad on national television, Cory found himself surrounded by a swarm of reporters' microphones, but his thoughts drifted far from the gridiron to a few days earlier, when a young man had threatened to jump off a building, and Cory was the first responder. After a long and intense exchange on the rooftop, the man had reached over and grabbed Cory's hand.

Cory recalls, "It was a moment where I said to myself, *Okay, I get it.* Being there to touch somebody's spirit was much more important to me than being surrounded by microphones. . . . I think we all have to do what we are called to do. For me, it was a matter of what fulfilled me the most and having the courage to be loyal to that calling no matter where that path leads."

He attended Oxford University as a Rhodes scholar and then Yale Law School but hadn't yet figured out how to put his talents and passion for service to use in the world. "I was pretty firm on what I didn't want to do," he says, "but I still didn't know how to manifest the desires I had. . . . I had a choice of going down a more traditional route or going my own way. I decided to invent myself."

Following long conversations with his mother and other close confidantes, he says that he asked himself "*What would be the wildest dream for myself—the largest thing that I could do that would make me feel that sense of fulfillment and contribution?* I decided I wanted to be part of a community in transformation. . . . I had this ambitious desire to go to the front lines of this struggle and fight." He envisioned himself finding the worst street in the entire city of Newark, New Jersey (not far from where he grew up), living there, and joining that effort. "I was really naïve at the time," he recalls, "but I think it was one of the smarter things I could have done."

In pursuit of his vision, Cory secured a modest fellowship and moved into the Brick Towers, one of Newark's toughest housing projects. A drug trade was flourishing across the street, anchored by a crack house. In his first month there, the body of someone who had been bludgeoned to death was found on a street corner, and Cory witnessed a shooting on his front steps. Then his life was threatened by the local drug lord.

"That night I had a real gut check," he recalls. "This guy had so convincingly scared me that I had to ask myself, *Is this worth dying for?*" He found strength in a quote from Edward Teller, which he paraphrases, "When you come to the end of all the light you know and you are about to step into the darkness, faith is knowing one of two things will happen. Either you find solid ground underneath you or God will send you people who will teach you how to fly."

Booker decided to stay and fight. Soon afterward, he met with the local tenant president, Virginia Jones, and offered to help, admittedly with a "touch of arrogance in addition to audacity." Looking back, he laughs. "I told her 'Hi, my name's Cory Booker, I'm a law student, ma'am, and I'm here to help you'. . . like I was a sheriff from an old Western. And she put me in my place." After Jones asked him what he saw around him and he described in plain terms the conditions of his impoverished neighborhood, she rebuked him: "You need to understand that the world you see out-side of you is a reflection of what you see inside of you. If you see only problems and darkness and despair, that's all it's ever going to be. If you are a person who sees hope and opportunity and the face of God, then you can be one with the people who make real change." And so began Cory's streetwise education.

In the ensuing months, he and Ms. Jones met with their neighbors at her kitchen table and collectively decided to form a coalition for community change. Substantially through their efforts, the crack house was torn down, the slum lord was con-victed, and a local business "adopted" a neighborhood school. Cory recalls, "It was a very powerful experience. I was sold. I knew what I was going to do . . . and my dreams got bigger and bolder. . . . [It] unleashed my belief in what was possible."

Leveraging its early wins, the Brick Towers Coalition began to effect change on a larger scale. Soon they realized they needed cooperation from the city government, but the local politicians were not on board, perhaps in large part because many of the biggest landowners were their major campaign contributors. The tenant group pressured Cory to throw his hat in the ring for city council to "take on the machine."

For Booker, this was another big "gut check." To run, he was going to have to give up his fellowship and income, sideline (and risk throwing away) the work that he had become so pas-sionate about, and spend six months trying to unseat a powerful incumbent—all in a place where politicians typically only leave office if they are being "buried or convicted." Racked by sleep-less nights and back spasms induced by stress, Booker recalls, "It was one of the most difficult decisions I've had to make. . . . Everything was going in the direction I had imagined, and now suddenly people were confronting me with evidence that some-thing else should be done on a bigger scale." One day, a friend challenged him, "Are you here to do what you want to do or to meet the needs of the community?"

And so he ran. Cory engaged in a bruising battle for a seat on the city council, defeating a four-time incumbent. He car-ried his independent streak and unconventional approach into office—living for five months in a motor home, parking on corners notorious for drug trafficking, and going on a ten-day hunger strike outside a housing project to protest open-air drug dealing. Though he proposed a number of bold initiatives, he was regularly outvoted (typically eight to one) by an entrenched city council. Stymied by the corrupt politics of the city, he decided to run for mayor against sixteen-year incumbent Sharpe James. After another nasty campaign (captured in the Academy Award–nominated documentary *Street Fight*), Mayor James prevailed with 53 percent of the vote.

Cory recommitted himself to the city and went on to found and direct Newark Now—a grassroots, citywide civic leadership program that is still thriving today—and to run again for mayor in 2006. Seeing the strong support behind Booker, James recognized the writing on the wall and withdrew from the race. At thirty-seven, Mayor Cory Booker was finally in a position to enact systemic change for the city and its people.

Now in office, he faces enormous challenges. A death threat issued by local gangs resisting his tough stance on crime resulted in a twenty-four-hour security detail. But his resolve has only been strengthened. "My life has been one long path," he says. "There are days when I get punched and knocked down, but I get up again and keep walking. The path has led in directions that I could never have anticipated . . . but I need to keep asking: *Am I dedicated to my values and my ideas? Am I acting courageously even when the path leads into pitch darkness?* I still need to walk down this path."

> *If one advances confidently in the direction of his*
> *dreams, and endeavors to live the life which he has*
> *imagined, he will meet with a success unexpected in*
> *common hours. He will pass an invisible boundary;*
> *new, universal, and more liberal laws will begin to*
> *establish themselves around and within him; and he*
> *will live with the license of a higher order of beings.*
> —HENRY DAVID THOREAU

"RAISING THE BAR"

"I felt trapped."

It had been ten years since Gary Erickson had launched the energy bar company Clif Bar & Co. The ups and downs of the company's start-up years had been exhilarating, but now Gary was pushed into a corner, beaten down, and about to sell the company that had been his happy obsession for the past decade.

Gary's partner had a 50 percent stake in the business, and she wanted out. As the market matured and the competition intensified, the ongoing risks were too much for her to bear. All of it was affecting Gary: he had stopped exercising, wasn't sleeping well, and was mired in stress. He recounts, "I was getting worn out. We needed money to grow the business. I was marooned and everybody would just beat me down. . . . Everybody was saying that the competition was going to kill us."

The industry was consolidating: all of Clif Bar's competitors were being bought by global corporations, and Power Bar now had the resources of Nestlé, the largest food company in the world. "My partner was literally having breakdowns in the office," he continues. "It was crazy. So I gave in and just said, '*That's it, let's just sell it.*'"

Selling would be lucrative. Gary was on the cusp of bringing in $60 million personally from the sale, but he was torn because this wasn't just a business to him.

The concept of the Clif Bar had come to him during an epic bike ride with his friend Jay over Mount Hamilton in northern California. It was supposed to be a 125-mile ride, but Jay had miscalculated the distance—badly. As they approached the 125-mile mark, they realized that they still had a punishing 50 miles to go. Gary was "bonking": his muscles were shutting down due to fatigue and a lack of nutrients. He "just couldn't eat another chewy, bland energy bar," so they found a 7-Eleven and he powered through a package of powdered-sugar donuts. Pushing into the final leg of the ride, he turned to Jay and announced, "I'm going to create a better-tasting energy bar."

That "epiphany ride," as he now calls it, led to a start-up sensation that took the nascent energy bar industry by storm. Living in a garage at the time with his dog, skis, climbing gear, bike, and two trumpets, he recruited his mother to help him gin up different recipes in the kitchen until they finally landed on one that was just right.

The first year, they racked up $700,000 in sales and had their products selling in seven hundred bike shops and hundreds of natural foods stores. From 1992, the company's revenues nearly doubled each year—to more than $100 million in 2002. Clif Bar—named after Gary's father, Clifford—became not only a lifestyle product but a grassroots phenomenon as they promoted their energy bars "at the point of passion": at climbing crags, bike events, marathons, triathlons, and more.

The power of his vision was not only in the market opportunity he spotted (and strategically tapped into) but in the authentic convergence of his passions that the product embodies. His core identity was wrapped up in his passion for music and the great outdoors as well as his family's love affair with good food. Looking back, he says that "the best ideas come out of extreme situations in unknown terrain, whether in cycling or in business. Pushing beyond what I think I can do creates an opening for new ideas. The bike epiphany was a purely intuitive moment. Yet it brought together three elements of my life in a way that made sense. . . . Successful entrepreneurs take who they are and what they already know and create surprising combinations."[1]

Gary's cooking heritage and enjoyment of good food can be traced to his Greek grandmother, Kalliope. Before starting Clif Bar, he had opened what he calls a "fresh and artisan" bakery in the Bay Area based on recipes from his mother and grandmother.

He was also a jazz fanatic. He had become enamored with jazz way back in the fifth grade, jammed in bands throughout high school and college, and even considered a career in music. "What I like about jazz is improvisation," he explains. "There is a discipline side of the improvisation and then there is a free-form part, and I think business is the same thing. . . . Having the skills to do it but then being able to risk your own melody or solo reminds me of being an entrepreneur. . . . Jazz has always been an influence in how I run my business."

The third point of convergence was his lifestyle, flowing from his love of outdoor adventure sports, the wilderness, and what he calls the "white road" approach. He grew up playing every sport known to man, and his whole family would frequently head to countless national parks for hiking, skiing, and more. Gary took up mountain and ice climbing, then bike racing, and later became a wilderness guide. "None of these things made a lot of money," he says, "but it didn't matter because I was living the lifestyle I wanted to live. I was living in the mountains and

climbing every day and hanging out with really cool people."
Eventually, he saved enough money after holding down three
jobs to travel around the world for a year. On a subsequent biking trip through the European Alps, he and a buddy found that
the "red roads" on the maps were full of traffic and congestion,
but the "white roads" were the smaller paths that led to adventure and risk. They always took the white roads.

Gary brought all those elements—good food, jazz, and the
"white road" approach—to Clif Bar. He had poured his heart and
soul into it. Now it was all about to end.

"It came down to the last minute," he says, "one last walk
around the block. That moment changed everything. I decided
I'm not going to do this." He returned to the office and sent the law-
yers home. "I felt the happiest I had felt in months," he recalls.
In his book, *Raising the Bar,* he elaborated: "I didn't know it at the
time, but my walk around the block exposed *the nature of things* to
me; it revealed what I wanted in a partnership, in the company,
in my life, and in my marriage."[2]

He was ecstatic, but the decision carried immense risk. To
honor his business partner's wishes, he had to buy her out.
"Instead of selling and walking away with $60 million for my half
of the business," he explains, "I was now keeping the company
but facing $70 million of debt financing to buy my partner out of
her half of the business." Facing what appeared to be a bottom-
less pit of debt and uncertainty, he resolved to take Clif Bar as
far down the "white road" path as possible and see where it led.
Staying private and in full control was key to staying on that road.

Gary's goal was "to create and sustain a business where people can live and experience life, not just where they go to make
a living. . . . I wanted to create a place where people had fun,
worked hard, and felt that their work had meaning."[3] Collectively,
they developed the company's "Five Aspirations" centered on sustaining their brands, business, people, community, and planet.

These are not just platitudes at Clif Bar. In many ways, the
company was designed by a life entrepreneur for life entrepreneurs. In the spirit of their aspirations, they created a collaborative culture that is disciplined, entrepreneurial, and playful. They
offer profit sharing for employees, sabbaticals, and a wellness
program, including an in-house gym, three full-time trainers,

and twenty fitness classes per week—during working hours. Employees get paid for staying in shape (two and a half hours of workout time per week) and are able to take a three-day weekend every other week. They built a theater in their headquarters, complete with a grand piano and Hammond organ, where they have their Wednesday night jam sessions. "Music is part of Clif Bar," says Gary. "People spend 2,080 hours a year at the workplace. We believe that if we provide meaningful work as well as something *beyond* work, people will do their jobs well *and* lead healthier, more balanced lives."[4]

Clif Bar also has a robust community service program, including a goal of over twenty paid hours of community volunteer work per person per year, and in 2006 launched the Clif Bar Family Foundation to provide financial support to grassroots organizations working to promote environmental restoration and conservation, sustainable food and agriculture, and an array of other social concerns. Several years ago the company went "green," with an aggressive sustainability initiative led by a staff ecologist.

This multifaceted approach is paying off. With high morale, a diversified line of energy bars (including Luna, the Whole Nutrition Bar for Women), and growing global brand recognition, the company has grown approximately 24 percent each year (compounded) for the past nine years to almost $150 million and shed all of its debt. The Clif Bar brand has become the number-one-selling organic energy and nutrition bar on the market.

Gary himself has managed to build this progressive enterprise while also maintaining an integrated life. He explains, "There is no separation of work and play. It's all together. . . . For me, the goal was to keep the lifestyle. I've been able to create a business that supports all the things I love to do." This includes prioritizing family time with his wife and children. They ski every weekend in the winter, travel in summer, mountain bike together, attend Clif events as a family, and recently completed a five-thousand-mile biodiesel R.V. (recreational vehicle) "white road" trip to educate their children and the Clif Bar customer community on the potential of biofuels.

Today he and his wife Kit are focused on maintaining the company's "mojo," as he calls it. In 2004 they started the Clif Bar

Family Winery and Farm, supporting organic farming in their community. "Entrepreneurs bring their life stories into business," says Gary. "Entrepreneurialism is more about a spirit, passion, desire, and way of being than about innate gifts and abilities. It is the willingness to tackle first ascents—climbing new routes."[5] His recipe for living his dreams? "Just enjoy it. It doesn't take that much to be really happy. Why not be happy today?"

> We must not forget that only a very few people
> are artists in life; that the art of life is the most
> distinguished and rarest of all the arts.
> —CARL JUNG

CREATING BRIGHT HORIZONS

Having grown up in a little farming village in the Finger Lake area of central New York, Linda Mason recalls, "A big early influence in my life was my father. Every few years, he would take a few months off his practice and go to a country in the developing world and volunteer as a doctor in Central America and Africa. I just hung on his stories when he came back."

Inspired by that novel combination of adventure and humanitarian work, Linda sought to push the boundaries of her own life. She moved to Paris after college to study another passion, music, at the Rachmaninoff Conservatory. At the time she "had no objective in mind as far as what my future would hold—no plan whatsoever. I mainly was thinking about what kind of adventure I would have."

She then volunteered for a non-profit that worked with North African refugees. "I became very interested in humanitarian work," she recalls, "but I had no skill, and not too many humanitarian groups have a need for classical pianist or art history majors. So I thought maybe I'll go back and get a management degree."

While in business school, she interned with the consulting firm Booz Allen Hamilton, which offered her a full-time international position when she graduated. But circumstances intervened. She explains, "That was the year that the Vietnamese invaded Cambodia and ousted the Khmer Rouge, and hundreds of thousands of refugees fled to the border of Thailand. It was in the newspaper every day." She decided to defer her consulting work and instead go to Cambodia with two classmates, Neal Keny and Roger Brown. The idea was to work in refugee camps for the summer and write case studies on the management of relief operations. For her, it was "the sense of adventure and this draw to humanitarian work."

That's when her world got turned upside down: "Ten days after we arrived, our refugee camps were attacked by the Vietnamese and the whole area turned into a war zone. The needs became much, much greater, and several organizations withdrew. The organizations that stayed had an enormous crisis on their hands, so we decided to extend our stay." Linda and Roger ended up writing a book, called *Rice, Rivalry, and Politics: Managing Cambodian Relief,* on the management of the relief effort—and they also started dating.

When the year came to a close, she honored her commitment to Booz Allen Hamilton and traded in interviews with ambassadors and jungle warlords for a suit and an office. She recalls, "When I returned to the States, I was working on the forty-fifth floor in midtown Manhattan wearing stockings, heels, and a suit. It was a shocking transition. . . . I threw myself into it, but I could never really get inspired."

At a New Year's gathering a couple of years later, a friend asked the revelers to reflect back on the year and their accomplishments. Linda remembers, "I looked back and was mainly depressed. I made a ton of money, I worked eighty hours a week, but I didn't really feel that I had accomplished much of anything. I felt fairly empty."

Linda and Roger—now married—concluded, *This is not what we want to do with our life.* That led her to a seeking phase in which she started examining, thinking, and becoming very open to what was around her. At the time, there was a severe famine in Sudan and Ethiopia, and she and Roger were drawn to helping. Through her former classmate, Neal Keny, they learned that a relief organization was looking for a team to go to Africa.

Linda explains, "The head of Save the Children called us and invited us to meet, so we flew down to New York to his apartment on a Sunday afternoon. He had just come back from Sudan and Ethiopia and painted this picture of incredible human devastation. He asked us to go over and launch a program for them.

Then he said, 'But I need to know by tomorrow.' We walked out of his apartment and looked at each other and decided on the spot. It seemed very impetuous but actually it wasn't at all. We had been open to something like this. Three weeks later, we were in Khartoum."

Save the Children had already raised $2 million for this initiative, but it had never operated in that part of Africa, so Linda and Roger raised another $10 million and built an emergency famine relief organization in Sudan. As she recalls, "It was intense. The crisis was enormous. We put a great deal of thought into creating a strong organization that was very entrepreneurial. We hired people and trained and developed them, and it became very large. We served about four hundred thousand famine victims. We had committed to staying there until the first good harvest. It was a job that was 24×7 in very tough conditions. . . . When we returned to the States, we were pretty burned out."

They didn't know what would come next, but they set certain goals for the next chapter of their lives: they wanted to create an organization on their own, do it together, and do something that would make a difference in people's lives. With that in mind, they started taking "long walks with a pen and pad in hand and just dreaming." Through an old friend from their consulting days, they were turned on to the idea of starting a network of work-site child-care centers, a type of business that didn't exist at the time. For weeks, they analyzed it methodically, ultimately deciding that it could work.

The launch of Bright Horizons Family Solutions corporation was both invigorating and taxing. As Linda recounts:

> We were very idealistic and wanted to make a difference, and we were going to do it quickly. Then we had a long, long period of struggle where we just hit brick wall after brick wall, and it took five times as long to get the company up than we had forecasted. It was really an idea before its time and it was hard to get support, but we stuck to our guns. . . . The company did almost collapse a few times. We were also starting a family at this very time and that's not something I recommend to beginning entrepreneurs . . . but we stepped into it and I think having each other made a difference. If one of us started to lose our resolve, the other one could hold you up. A strong partnership really helped us through those tough times

and helped us keep focused on our original vision, and now we have done it.

Today, Bright Horizons operates more than six hundred day-care centers in the United States and Europe. Not long after launching, Linda and Roger also noticed that no one in the industry was serving the growing underclass of homeless children, so "though it made no logical sense" at the time—given the start-up challenges of the parent company—they launched Horizons for Homeless Children, a non-profit that has since created over one hundred play spaces for children in homeless shelters and three full-service child-care centers for homeless children.

One of the biggest challenges for Linda had to do with work-life balance. Linda recalls, "Here I was having a baby while I was running a child-care organization. . . . I had enormous support and great child care, but it was so difficult to be a parent and run this organization. . . . When I wasn't with my baby, I felt guilty. When I wasn't at work, I felt like I was letting things down there. It was a huge struggle, and I wanted to be great at both—to be a wonderful devoted mother and a great entrepreneur." She later wrote a book, *Working Mother's Guide to Life*, to help other working moms navigate that maze.

Looking back, Linda believes that allowing herself to have seeking phases while also remaining open to new opportunities that fit with her values has been essential to creating a life of adventure, service, and fulfillment—from Paris to the Cambodian border to Khartoum to the brighter horizons she and Roger have created for thousands of children, including their own.

> *Life is either a daring adventure or nothing at all.*
> —Helen Keller

Three stories, three lives—all different, all inspirational and instructive. As we have seen in each of these accounts, leading an extraordinary life entails a willingness to take chances and push beyond the boundaries of what is comfortable. Think back to Cory's decision to move to Newark, face real danger, and run for office against an entrenched opponent. Or Gary's decision to turn away a lucrative opportunity to sell his company in order to build a stronger organization aligned with his values. Or Linda and Roger's decision to leave comfortable consulting careers to dedicate themselves to humanitarian work in Africa and child-care support in the United States.

Life entrepreneurs also draw strength from close relationships and build healthy support systems to help them accomplish their vision. Think about the early influence of Cory's parents and the important lesson Cory learned from Virginia Jones. For Gary, strength and inspiration came from the team he built at Clif Bar and the support he draws from his wife and children. For Linda and Roger, it was the commitment to stick together through the toughest challenges and thus grow stronger in the process.

In the end, our resolve to live our life "out loud" or as a "daring adventure" must come from within, first by understanding—and honoring—who we really are. We explain how in the next chapter.

CHAPTER THREE

DISCOVERING CORE IDENTITY

Each man had only one genuine vocation—to find the way to himself.
—HERMANN HESSE

Setting out on the path of the life entrepreneur, any of us may wander astray without a clear sense of who we are. The first step on the path is discovering what we call our *core identity*, our authentic essence. We can have all sorts of external amenities—career, wealth, power, personality, looks, approval, admiration, and more—but without a grounding in something deeper, the journey will leave us wanting. "If the foundation is weak," says the Chinese proverb, "the fortress will fall."

What does it mean to discover our core identity? How do we go about doing it? This is no small question. It may be the question of the ages.

Drawing on recent literature in the field, especially in psychology, as well as our interviews and personal experiences, we have concluded that one's core identity is informed by three external elements (personal history, current circumstances, and relationships) and three internal elements (needs, strengths, and passions). It is at the convergence of these elements that we find our values and purpose, the essence of our core identity (see Figure 3.1).

Figure 3.1. Core Identity.

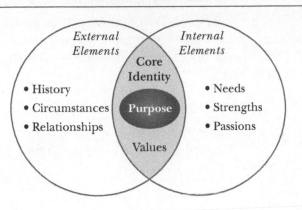

Note: Exercises addressing each of the elements of core identity can be found on this book's companion website, www.lifeentrepreneurs.com.

To discover our core identity, we must explore how these elements manifest themselves in our lives. The importance of this is almost universally overlooked, despite the sages and leaders throughout history who have urged us to know ourselves deeply.[1] Leadership expert Warren Bennis has said that "letting the self emerge is the essential task of leaders." He cites a study of the advice that top executives would give to younger ones, in which three recommendations surfaced: first, take advantage of every opportunity; second, aggressively search for meaning; and third, *know yourself.* Authors Bill George and Peter Sims call it finding your "true north"—"the internal compass that guides you successfully through life. It represents who you are as a human being at your deepest level. It is your orienting point."[2]

How can we achieve such self-awareness? The process is one of "dis-covering," or removing the layers of sediment that obstruct our view—layers of ego, pride, ambition, and expectations that so often bury our own identity. It is a process that requires not only reflection but also *action.* Knowing oneself is usually an outcome of an iterative process of introspection, action, change, and reflection.

I. EXTERNAL ELEMENTS

There are three primary external elements that inform the core of who we are: personal history, current circumstances, and relationships. In this section we treat each of these in turn.

PERSONAL HISTORY

> *Everything that happens to you is your teacher.*
> *The secret is to sit at the feet of your own life and be*
> *taught by it.*
> —POLLY B. BERENDS

Jael Kampfe, now in her thirties, grew up in Red Lodge, Montana, just south of the sprawling, old-style ranch that her great-grandfather purchased in 1901—twelve thousand acres of cattle ranching country rimmed by snow-capped peaks. She recounts, "He was a visionary, and it is amazing to me to be living as part of an intact legacy. Part of entrepreneurship is creating something physical out of something internal. This ranch is a physical manifestation of my grandfather and his vision."

That setting provided her with a sense of possibility, challenge, and self-reliance, as well as big skies to dream under. Her father was prone to rounding up the whole family and flying them to Alaska for a month with no plan. As a young girl, she was taught to fight her own battles: "Part of that is never having an option to do anything but go through it. The harder it gets, the more you work to figure it out. When you get through it, no one can take it away from you."

That lesson became tragically necessary when her father died in a plane crash when she was eleven. To her, it was the "end of our world." With newfound determination, she became an accomplished dancer and attended college on scholarship and from there earned an Echoing Green fellowship to edit a book on the language of the Lakota Indians.

It turned out to be "a transformative experience that changed my life," she says. While living on the Indian reservation, she was struck by the pressing needs of the Lakota people. Before long she decided to act, creating the Four Times Foundation to invest in Native American entrepreneurs through an equity-based venture capital investment model. (The name comes from the Lakota understanding of giving, which teaches that we should give what we have freely, trusting that in time it will come back to us four times over.) The foundation worked on five reservations, among the poorest communities in the nation.

As her organization grew, Jael found herself at a crossroads. In addition to running the foundation, she was dancing in a professional troupe. She soon realized that it was time to choose. "I knew I was capable of dancing on that level," she recalls, "but I realized that it didn't feed my spirit. It wasn't creative enough. I was someone else's paint as a dancer, and I wanted to be the one holding the brush. What the foundation gave me was the ability to create something out of nothing."

That decision-making process allowed her to understand her values more deeply and recognize how they were shaped by growing up on the ranch. "My roots are a driving force for who I am," she explains. "I know who I am. The more we try to be something we're not, the less successful we'll be. How do we capitalize on who we are so that it allows us to do more?"

Today, she is connected directly to her roots as the family ranch's first female manager, and she is bringing an entrepreneur's touch to it all. Not content to stick with the cattle drives, she is planning to bring high school girls to the ranch for a "cowgirl entrepreneurial boot camp"—helping the young women tap into their leadership potential through the rugged beauty of her expansive backyard.

Through Jael's story, we can witness the importance of our personal history in our lives. Our history is our life story, our personal narrative. It encompasses where we come from, our experiences, and what we have done with our lives. We are wise to consider how our personal history affects, directs, or even corrupts our current life path. According to Christina Baldwin, "We become ourselves based on a combination of life events and how we respond to them."[3]

It may sound easy, but precious few of us mine the chapters of our personal story to inform and enrich our days. Most of us glance fleetingly at our history through a rearview mirror while charging into the future. Author Kevin Cashman has lamented that "many of us know more about our favorite vacation spot, sports team, or running shoes than we do about ourselves. In order to break out of old patterns and grow as a whole person, we need to answer the 'Who am I?' question. . . . I think the reason most people think they know themselves well is that their experience of their inner world is restricted to very narrow boundaries."[4]

To avoid getting lost, it is essential to know ourselves in full and embrace our entire personal narrative, not just the chapters stamped with a smiley face. For many, the most significant chapters are those marked by struggle—with missed opportunities, personal failures, lost bearings, grave illnesses, or painful losses. "In the midst of winter," said the philosopher Albert Camus, "I finally learned that there was in me an invincible summer."

Sometimes it is hard to be more than the embodiment of our history, the cumulative inertia of past decisions and experiences brought forward into the present, weighing on our shoulders. What does it take to shrug that weight off, to heave it aside and start anew? We must recognize the truth of our history without letting ourselves become captive to it. Our personal history should inform but not confine our present path.

We always maintain the ability to change the trajectory of our lives. Sometimes that requires examining our history, seeking a deeper understanding of what has happened and why, and probing for lessons. In *True North,* George and Sims suggest that "successful leadership takes conscious development and requires being true to your life story. . . . The difference with authentic leaders lies in the way they frame their stories. Their life stories provide the context for their lives, and through them they find the passion and inspiration to make an impact in the world."[5]

CURRENT CIRCUMSTANCES

Six months before we interviewed her, Bridget Bradley Gray was in a very different place. As a rising leader at an education non-profit in Washington, D.C., she was on a promising career trajectory. But it was her prior experience with starting and running a small business, importing Vietnamese handbags, that put a sparkle in her eye. She loved working in a creative trade with energetic people and being challenged to make all kinds of decisions.

The hard part was the inner struggle that arose from her conflicting passions and values. Her strong sense of service and social justice was deeply ingrained. Her career in education entailed important work, but sometimes it left her wanting more. She was torn, in part because her current circumstances urged caution and stasis. She was newly married and hoping to start a family soon. And she looked around and saw friends with high-powered careers. But her restless energy persisted.

From this swirling confusion, a new idea emerged that had real possibility: a consignment shop for expectant mothers. It could be a way for her to create and run a new enterprise while also helping expectant mothers, many on low incomes, meet their basic needs. The idea was tantalizing. But how could she turn her back on the career in education she had built, only to gamble it on something so new and unknown? She would be leaping off a career cliff.

As she puzzled through her dilemma, she found strong support from her husband, David, and from a new mentor who had a nearby boutique shop. She decided to go for it. Days before her new store was to open, Bridget and David were in there at all hours of the night fixing leaks and making sure the space was worthy of her dream. Wiggle Room opened without a hitch.

The significance of this change in her life is not so much the business itself as it is the fact that she courageously chose a new direction in her life after listening to her inner voice and tuning out or at least muffling the outer ones. Still, her new path is not without challenges. When asked about her current concerns, she identifies "the challenge of maintaining balance in our lives—anything that pulls us away from spending time on what we love doing." Looking back, she says, "I think I've always had a strong sense of who I am, but allowing myself to be that person is more recent."

Bridget's story speaks to the power of the current circumstances in our lives—our community, age, health, marital status, occupation, income, and more. Think of the young mother caught in the cross fire of wanting to be a good mom but also having burning professional ambitions, or the retired executive yearning to make up for lost years of blazing intensity at the office but not wired for conventional retirement. Think of the talented young go-getter ready to take on the world but not yet certain about what to do with her life, feeling the seductive pull of all her friends landing prestigious jobs with hefty pay packages.

Sometimes our circumstances are favorable, with new people entering our lives and new doors opening. Life entrepreneurs leverage those opportunities into something even greater. Other times, it is the opposite. But we should be wary of the false security that sometimes accompanies success. Author Po Bronson warns, "Failure's hard, but success is far more dangerous. If you're successful at the wrong thing, the mix of praise and money and opportunity can lock you in forever."

The life entrepreneur sees her current circumstances with clarity and honestly assesses the distance between her current circumstances and her future dreams, then resolves to close the gap. Like Bridget, she is wise to turn to her close relationships for a little help along the way.

RELATIONSHIPS

> Well, what are you? What is it about you that
> you have always known as yourself? What are you
> conscious of in yourself: your kidneys, your liver,
> your blood vessels? No. However far you go in your
> memory it is always some external manifestation of
> yourself where you came across your identity: in the
> work of your hands, your family, in other people.
> And now, listen carefully. You in others—this is
> what you are, this is what your consciousness has
> breathed, and lived on, and enjoyed throughout your
> life, your soul, your immortality—your life in others.
> —BORIS PASTERNAK, DOCTOR ZHIVAGO

Our relationships—the interpersonal connections we may have with a spouse, partner, family, friends, mentors, colleagues, and others—deeply pervade our core identity. Our identity is a pale shadow without the people in our lives. According to the

Zulu saying, *umuntu ngumuntu ngabantu:* "A person is a person because of other people."

Here we come to one of the central themes of this book: life entrepreneurship is not a solo journey. It is through the people in our lives that we find opportunities to serve, learn, grow, share wisdom, find solidarity, and celebrate what we can accomplish together. The authors of this book can testify to the unmistakable impact our spouses, family, friends, mentors, teachers, coaches, and close colleagues have had on our lives.

Every step in the path of the life entrepreneur can be taken with others, and all throughout we can be sure we will need help along the way. These relationships not only inform our identity but also become a wellspring of happiness. According to economist Richard Easterlin, it is spending quality time with loved ones and friends that makes people happier, not earning more money. Research has shown that happy people have more friends.[6] But these relationships are worthwhile in and of themselves, and it is only through them that we can fully discover our core identity.

Of course, not all relationships are the kind that leave footprints. Aristotle said that there are three types of friendship: friendships based on utility (where a person is useful to us), friendships based on pleasure (company we enjoy, making us laugh), and friendships based on virtue (or "friends in the good," lifting us to strive and become better people)—the highest form of friendship. It is the latter that leave their etchings in our hearts and remind us of who we are.

Time and time again, we have seen the imprint left by those friends in the good. Think of Cory Booker and the mentoring he received from Virginia Jones. Think of Linda Mason and Roger Brown and how they lead a life of adventure together. Think of Stacey Boyd and Scott Hamilton and little Gracie and how they decided to fast-forward to their dreams today. Think of Christopher and the university president who taught him about being *un empresario cultural*—and Gregg and Professor Roth, who taught him about living the questions on the way to the good life. They all speak to how much who we are is "our life in others."

II. INTERNAL ELEMENTS

Following the three external elements of personal history, current circumstances, and relationships, we now turn to the three internal elements that inform core identity: our needs, strengths, and passions.

NEEDS

Our needs in life show up in many forms. Each of us has our own permutation of needs, but psychologist Abraham Maslow famously developed a classic "hierarchy of needs," depicted in Figure 3.2.

There is a sequence to these needs, requiring that we satisfy the lower needs before we can fully transition to the higher ones. Often, there is a tension between our practical *needs* (often related to financial security) and our *wants* (such as an ideal job or dream house). We frequently fail to distinguish between our needs and wants, as when we define a desired standard of living

FIGURE 3.2. MASLOW'S HIERARCHY OF NEEDS.

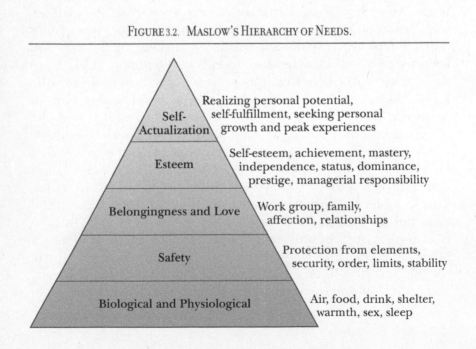

for ourselves based on external factors or comparisons with our peers.

The challenge is to maintain a realistic approach to material concerns that addresses needs and wants reasonably. We should be wary of the "doom loop" that keeps us in jobs we do not like in order to meet our "needs." In our interview with Seth Goldman, founder of Honest Tea, he spoke about the typical trajectory of college to career to home, marriage, and children—with all the attendant obligations—and how that trajectory prevents us from taking risks that can catalyze breakthroughs in our lives. To avoid that trap, he lives a Spartan life so that he and his family can maintain the freedom to leap when exciting opportunities arise, as with the organic tea company that he started out of his kitchen with a former professor. (More on that later.)

According to Maslow, our needs culminate in a quest for self-actualization. He explains, "Even if all these needs are satisfied, we may still often (if not always) expect that a new discontent and restlessness will soon develop unless the individual is doing what he is fitted for. A musician must make music, an artist must paint, a writer must write if he is to be ultimately at peace with himself. What a man can be, he must be. This need we call self-actualization."

This speaks to why discovering our core identity is essential. Too many people lead a life that doesn't cohere with their authentic essence. Too many see their true identity buried by external pressures, expectations, or circumstances, squashing their potential for authenticity and self-actualization.

Not all of our needs are healthy. If half the battle is knowing what our needs are, the other half is what has been called "managing our hungers."[7] These are the tendencies that can get us into trouble through inappropriate, excessive, compulsive, or addictive behavior, such as a thirst for admiration, wealth, or power. Albert Camus reminded us that "there is no sun without shadow, and it is essential to know the night."

In *Authentic Leadership,* Bill George points out that "being true to the person you were created to be means accepting your faults as well as using your strengths. Accepting your shadow side is an essential part of being authentic. The problem comes when people are so eager to win the approval of others that they try to cover their shortcomings and sacrifice their authenticity to gain the respect and admiration of their associates."[8] This was the trap Chip Conley of Joie de Vivre fell into, creating a "hologram" of himself to gain acceptance before embracing who he really was. We will address this further in Chapter Eight in the section on "avoiding the pitfalls."

Of course, we also have needs that are healthy and positive, and these are often primary drivers of our strengths.

STRENGTHS

> *The man who is born with a talent which he was*
> *meant to use finds his greatest happiness in using it.*
> —GOETHE

According to Albert Wiseman, Donald Clifton, and Curt Liesveld, coauthors of *Living Your Strengths,* a strength is "a powerful, productive combination of talent, skill, and knowledge." The fundamental building block is talent, which is innate. When that talent is enhanced by adding relevant skills and useful knowledge, a strength is born.

"If you're like most people," the authors posit, "you have grown up with the 'weakness prevention' model. You've been told that to become strong, successful, or truly serve . . . you must 'fix' your weaknesses. . . . That thinking is just plain wrong. . . . The evidence is overwhelming: You will be most successful in whatever you do by building your life around your greatest natural abilities rather than your weaknesses."[9]

Unfortunately, we live in a culture obsessed with celebrating underdogs and overcoming deficits, perversely urging people to take "the path of *most* resistance."[10] Many people waste precious time doing things they're no good at or trying to turn a weakness into a strength instead of creating a capacity for excellence out of existing competencies. Consider the following:

- In 2006, only 14 percent of workers reported that they spend their days playing to their strengths.
- Only 37 percent of workers from five leading industrial nations said that building their strengths would help them be more successful on the job.

- A whopping 63 percent believed that fixing their weaknesses would help.[11]

For the life entrepreneur, there are four implications of the research on strengths and weaknesses:

- We should leverage our strengths and avoid working in areas of weakness.
- We should seek partners and colleagues who have different strengths and who compensate for our weaknesses.
- We shouldn't become complacent about our existing strengths; instead, we should build complementary skill sets off our current strengths.
- We should continually seek ways to deploy our strengths in service of a worthy endeavor—preferably something we are passionate about.[12]

However, there is an important caveat: though we should avoid working in areas of weakness, we cannot ignore our weaknesses. They are important because they can derail us if we don't address them. As mentioned earlier, we must become acquainted with not only our better angels and strengths but also our "shadow side" and weaknesses so we have a clear and unfiltered sense of who we truly are.

PASSIONS

> Don't worry about what the world needs. Ask what
> makes you come alive and do that. Because what the
> world needs are people who have come alive.
> —HOWARD THURMAN

Our passions are the things that consume us with palpable emotion. The term comes from the Latin word *passio*, which means "suffering."

The coauthors of *Success Built to Last*, Jerry Porras, Stewart Emery, and Mark Thompson, conducted more than two hundred interviews and surveyed nearly four hundred enduringly successful people worldwide over ten years. Their work revealed that "loving what you do" is a necessary condition for success. Albert Schweitzer recognized this decades ago when he said, "Success is not the key to happiness. Happiness is the key to success. If you love what you are doing, you will be successful." The trick is not so much *having* passions as *finding* them: What makes us come alive? What do we get lost in? According to the *Success Built to Last* coauthors:

> Much is said today about the importance of loving what you do, but most people simply don't buy it. Sure, it would be nice to do what you love, but as a practical matter, most people don't feel they can afford such a luxury. . . . Listen up—here's some really bad news: It's dangerous not to do what you love. The harsh truth is that if you don't love what you're doing, you'll lose to someone who does! For every person who is half-hearted about their work or relationships, there is someone else who loves what they're half-hearted about. This person will work harder and longer. They will outrun you.[13]

Gerald Chertavian of Year Up found his passion in mentoring young people in need. He says "That's who I am at my core, what I love. I mean, if a young person calls me and says, 'Hey, can you help me? Can you listen to me?' I can't say no to that. It's almost physically impossible for me to say no."

Billionaire investor Warren Buffet once remarked, "If there is any difference between you and me, it may simply be that I get up every day and have a chance to do what I love to do, every day. If you want to learn anything from me, this is the best advice I can give you."

Author Curt Rosengren believes that bringing passion into our lives is "insanely simple" because it springs from simple authenticity. He defines passion as "the energy that comes from bringing more of *you* into what you do. In essence, passion comes from being who you are."[14] We should periodically gauge how much passion we have in our life and work, taking stock of areas where we are running low.

Let's be clear, though: it isn't enough to indulge our passions in life and call it a day. According to a recent study, it is misguided to think that simply doing the work we love will automatically result in happiness, achievement, and significance.

Our passions notwithstanding, we still feel conflicting desires, such as the tension between work and home.[15] The key is to be aware of our needs, passions, and other dimensions of an integrated life—such as family, work, happiness, health, and community—and live in such a way that each element receives its due according to the importance we place on it. This equation is a tricky—but important—one to solve. As we saw with Bridget and her decision to launch Wiggle Room while starting a family, the point is to choose deliberately, rather than adopting an approach by default or in deference to others.

III. Core Identity

Our core identity is informed by the external and internal elements covered above. At the convergence of those elements we find our values, which then help us uncover our purpose. We now address values and purpose in turn, first by seeing how a Colorado-based social entrepreneur placed values and purpose at the forefront of his life and work.

When he was on the Mekong River as a twenty-three-year-old navy officer in the Vietnam War serving on a support ship for various river patrol craft, John Horan-Kates had a flash of insight about what he would do next with his life. He envisioned a return to Colorado, a place that he had fallen in love with before he left for war, to become the marketing director at the Vail ski resort. He figured that would combine his strengths in marketing with his passion for skiing and the mountains. He wrote it down on a slip of paper as he traversed the river.

After his tour of duty, he honored that inspiration and led the marketing efforts for Vail Associates. Now a thirty-year resident of the Vail Valley, he has also run his own company and established and led the Vail Valley Foundation, then the Vail Leadership Institute. A dedicated servant of his community, John is always looking for ways to continue improving it—as well as his own life.

He has made a point of reviewing and renewing his path in life at least once a year, evaluating who he is and where he is going to ensure that he isn't just drifting. He calls it the "annual look." He has been doing it every year since 1977. Each

December, he reviews what he did the previous year in the areas of his life that matter most to him, assessing how he is doing in terms of his purpose, values, and goals. He also revisits these during the course of the year to hold himself accountable.

Today, he helps others do that and more through his work at the Vail Leadership Institute. Here's a man who is familiar with his core identity. He has articulated his values ("faith, family, learning, serving, and community") and purpose ("to build spiritually based communities"), and he lives them every day.

VALUES

Our values are what we believe and stand for, our convictions about the things we deem to be most important in life. Billy Shore, founder and executive director of Share Our Strength, thinks about values as "going out and bearing witness to things that move you." In our interview, Montana rancher Jael Kampfe said, "I don't care what I do as long as I adhere to certain values."

Most world-class companies and non-profits go through an intensive process to discover their organizational values, but many people neglect to give it much thought personally. Often, we simply inherit values from our parents (who inherited them from their parents, and so on) or adopt the prevailing values of our friends, community, society, culture, or faith tradition without engaging with them personally.

That is a mistake. Although these can be valuable or even vital inputs, the process of discovering and "owning" our personal values is essential in building a robust foundation for healthy relationships, productive work, and a meaningful life. To do this, we must ask: *What is most important to me? What are my deeply held beliefs and principles? What do I value most in life? How will I conduct myself and treat people?*

Some people value family, friendship, learning, growth, and spirituality. Other people value achievement, vision, passion, empowerment, and collaboration. Still others value creativity, beauty, compassion, fun, and humor. Or wisdom and wholeness. Truth and integrity. Nature and stewardship.[16] As we sort through this, we are wise to consider not only *what* we value, but also *why*.

A helpful exercise on mapping personal values can be found on this book's website.

Once we articulate our values, the next important question is: How should our values guide the way we live? How will we bring these values into our daily lives?

Part of the challenge is to recognize when there's a gap between our values and behaviors. Are we true to our better angels? According to a *Harvard Business Review* analysis, the most common reasons for a gap between our convictions and our commitments are (1) staying entangled in commitments made in the past; (2) experiencing "commitment creep," in which we take too many things on; (3) becoming prisoners to other people's expectations; and (4) becoming prisoners of success.[17] David Gray ran the risk of that when his series of successes in life brought him to a White House job offer that was nearly impossible to turn down, yet it was in tension with his priorities at the time of faith and family. In the end, he made a courageous decision based on his values, including his belief about how he could best serve others. He could have been a prisoner of other people's expectations or of success, but it was his values that allowed him to integrate his convictions and commitments.

Mike Galgon, now in his thirties and living in Seattle, provides an example of someone whose values are integral to his life and work. He grew up running all sorts of small businesses, paid his way through college via the Reserve Officers Training Corps (ROTC), and became a navy diver, doing "cool, crazy things that a twenty-two-year-old guy should be doing." After serving as a naval officer, he signed up for the Volunteers in Service to America (VISTA) program as a full-time volunteer for a year in the inner city. "It was the thing that seemed like the biggest opportunity to make a difference and to learn a bunch," he recalls. "I wanted to know more about inner-city economic development and try to do some good. I was taken by the sense of giving something back." For him, this value of service led him to his first big step in blazing his own trail.

He says that while he was in graduate school he realized that "if you set off on a path where you're making a lot of money, it's hard to go back. What makes me happy is just creating something—having a notion of a need and being able to marshal people to go after it. You can do that inside bigger companies, but that start-up thing was what I'd done." At that point in his life, he was also recognizing his passions and how they fit with his strengths.

After getting his business degree, he decided, "I had to go back to Seattle, and I had to start a business." His vision was to create a company that resonated with his values of community and service. "My notion," he says, "was that if you could start and build a business that created a great place for people to work and build their lives, that would be a very successful enterprise. And you can work with really interesting people. You don't end up with six really smart people and a bunch of workers. You end up with two thousand smart people—team players, nice people—who all create value together." This arose from an unspoken value of collaboration.

His notion of how he could serve through this work morphed from the belief that the mission of the organization itself had to be targeted to direct service to a new notion: that "the way you set up and run your organization could be of service—business as service."

In 1997, while in his twenties, he cofounded aQuantive based on those values. It has since grown to become the parent company of several digital marketing services and technology companies, including Avenue A | Razorfish. His company went public in 2000 and in 2007 was acquired by Microsoft for more than $6 billion—at the time, the largest single acquisition in Microsoft's history.

Though he served as president for a while, he now serves as chief strategy officer, which allows him to "keep being an entrepreneur inside this business, because there are so many businesses to start," while he can also maintain a healthy lifestyle: "I get all the best part of starting a business without the grind," he says.

As a result, he is able to live according to his values of service, community, and relationships, spending a lot of time with his family and friends while also running, hiking, and biking through Seattle's waterfront hills and trails.

When asked to recount the lessons he has learned from his adventures in business, social, and life entrepreneurship, he says, "Don't care what anybody else thinks. If you find something that grabs your heart, go do that. It's every bit as entrepreneurial to go start a little VISTA program in the inner city as it is to start a big internet company. Don't get fooled that one's better than the other. And just know that we're really lucky. Don't get bigheaded about your successes, and don't get used by money. I think that's a big part of happiness as an entrepreneur—not to be taken by the ride."

Connecting to Something Deeper

Many of the people we interviewed emphasized the critical value of a spiritual grounding in their life journey, of connecting to something deeper.

Cory Booker, the dynamic young mayor of Newark, calls his spirituality "absolutely fundamental to who I am. My parents taught me to view myself not in a human context but in a spiritual context, which allowed me to see myself as part of a larger spiritual universe. I have a reservoir of strength that is limitless if I am able to draw on that and connect with other people."

In our interviews, we observed three patterns of how spirituality shows up in people's lives, affecting their outlook and values:

- *Belief or faith in a higher power.* Often, this belief informed or even defined their values and helped them get beyond the trappings of their ego.
- *Moments of transcendence.* When we are employing our strengths in areas of passion, connecting deeply with others, and making worthy contributions, we can experience moments of enlightenment or transcendence. "There is this moment," recalls David Carmel of StemCyte, "where you are doing the thing that you wanted to do. They were moments that I felt closer to God. . . . It's important to find those transcendental moments when you feel you are completely in your element." Paul Nasrani of Adirondack Creamery called this "the hand of God" in his life: "As soon as you get active," he observed, "all of a sudden the spontaneous opportunities come out of nowhere. . . . The overall theme is this undying faith that, if you're active and doing your best, then what you need will be provided to you."

- *Pursuit of a calling.* David Gray felt called to the ministry as a way to serve others while also continuing his own spiritual journey. According to Kim Smith of the NewSchools Venture Fund, "I am not a religious person, but I have at many times in my life felt that I had a certain sort of calling. . . . It's not religious for me, but it is sort of spiritual. You have a certain set of opportunities, you land in a certain place. *What are you going to make of that? Are you going to step up or not?* My calling has always been about using everything I have to give tools to kids who are not going to get them otherwise to thrive."

For John Horan-Kates, spirituality is about all three of these patterns. He builds spirituality into everything that he does. During our interview with author Karin Weber, she said that her spiritual psychology studies "taught me to recognize that we are spiritual beings having a human experience, rather than the reverse. . . . It's a connection with a higher something. I don't know what that is—God or spirit or nature—but when you're in the flow of it you know it. It appeals to the highest standards by which we can live. In our everyday encounters, we have the opportunity to draw ourselves and those around us up or down."

For many, discussions of values—and core identity—are meaningless without spirituality. It can lead us to values of love, hope, connectedness, generosity, contribution, and more. Today, even as rising generations are questioning religious institutions with greater frequency, many are embracing spirituality as essential and defining elements of their lives, each in their own way.

> *The spiritual life is not a special career, involving abstraction from the world of things. It is a part of every man's life; and until he has realized it, he is not a complete human being, has not entered into possession of all his powers.*
> —EVELYN UNDERHILL, AUTHOR

Faith in Action

When she was ten, Inez Russell was touched by her own personal angel. "My grandmother taught me a lot about God," she recounts. "When I went to see her, we would go visit people.

We visited people in hospitals, nursing homes, and shut-ins. We would read the Bible to them, hug them, run errands for them, whatever they couldn't do. She believed that everybody had this responsibility. To her it was like breathing or walking. You just helped people who needed help. It was something she did all the time. It was just part of her, so natural. To me, my grandma was faith in action."

Through the years, Inez became a wife, mother, Sunday school teacher, and grandmother herself, and she built a successful career in the corporate world. As she would volunteer in various capacities and get to help people, she kept wondering: *What if this could be my job?*

One day, she was visiting a family member in the hospital when she heard a woman crying in a nearby room. The woman was by herself and was terribly afraid that she was about to die alone. Inez started visiting her regularly and they became friends. Inez began seeing big changes in the woman's outlook—and health. This wasn't lost on the hospital staff, who quickly steered her to other lonely patients.

That is when Inez started getting bombarded with stories about elderly people in need. "Every time I picked up a newspaper or turned on the television or radio, I just constantly heard about it." She looked around for organizations to address the problem but couldn't find any. "I finally reached a point where I said, *Okay, I will do this.*" And so she started Friends for Life, a charity that would serve elderly people in need.

At first, it was just her in a borrowed office with borrowed furniture. She recruited volunteers to visit people in hospitals and nursing homes.

"There was a lot of time spent responding to need. Everything we did seemed to reveal more needs. We found one lady sitting in the dark because all the lightbulbs in her house had burned out. So we started a lightbulb-changing program. We found one lady who had been stuck in her house for five years because she didn't have a wheelchair ramp, so we started a ramp-building program. . . . I went to visit a lady, found her sitting on her porch steps, crying. She had ants crawling on her. She kept saying, 'I don't know what to do, I don't know what to do.' When she would get up from her porch and try to walk, she would get lost. She had dementia. All her family had moved away. She didn't have anybody."

Today, Friends for Life serves nearly four thousand people a year in eighteen counties with the help of two thousand volunteers. They have programs for minor household repair, money management, music and art therapy, therapeutic gardening, Gifts for Grannies and Grandpas (like Toys for Tots), an Intergenerational Care Center, and an educational therapy program for children with learning disabilities.

As Inez reflects, "I knew this would work, but I didn't know how far it would go. . . . I learned to have faith and keep helping people. . . . Before Friends for Life, I wanted to know what I was doing here. Now I understand that my whole life was preparing me to do this work. I believe that this is what I am supposed to be doing."

PURPOSE

At the center of core identity is purpose, our reason for being. We can think of it as our calling, our own personal mission. It answers the age-old question: *Why am I here?* When we are clear about our purpose, or at least working toward it, our lives come together in powerful ways. According to Fyodor Dostoyevsky, "The secret of man's being is not only to live but to have something to live for."

As with values, many organizations go through a systematic process to discover their purpose (typically called their mission statement). The blockbuster book *Built to Last* found that "the essence of greatness does not lie in cost cutting, restructuring, or the pure profit motive. It lies in people's dedication to building companies around a sense of purpose—around core values that infuse work with the kind of meaning that goes beyond just making money."[18]

This also applies to people. In fact, the authors of the follow-up book, *Success Built to Last,* say that if there is one secret they have found in their study of hundreds of enduringly successful people, it is that each of us needs to "create a life that matters." Author and leadership expert Richard Leider asked a wide-ranging group of adults over age sixty-five the following: "If you could live your life over again, what would you do differently?" The three themes that emerged were: "Be more reflective. Be more courageous. Be clear earlier about purpose."[19]

If we lack purpose, we lose connection with our true nature and become externally driven, generating discontent or even angst. Because purpose can be so elusive, we often duck the big question and look for ways to bury that discontent, most often through "busyness," distraction, or worse. Leider has identified common obstacles to identifying purpose: the assumption that having purpose means doing something completely original; the misconception that only a few special people have true purpose in their lives; and the idea that purpose is nice but impractical—that we're just too busy to address it.[20]

How do we know when we have found our purpose? It has been said that the soul is like a well reaching down to the water source, a connector to the divine. If the connection is made—or broken—we'll know it. When the connection is made, our lives start to assume coherence—even the parts that had previously felt disjointed. Our lives reflect an inherent wholeness.

Attention should be paid to how we go about discovering purpose. For some, purpose is likely to unfold through deep reflection. True purpose just sits there, hidden, waiting for the time when we are ready for it. For others, purpose is more likely to be discovered through a more active process, with a dynamic interplay between action and reflection. We must each find a process that works for us. The point is to work toward it as best we can, not letting uncertainty prevent us from living our lives in the meantime.

Most of us assume that our job is to figure out what to do with our lives and then go do it and hope for the best. But sometimes we find ourselves wrestling with a new question: *What does life want from us?* In the end, the task is not *finding* our purpose but *uncovering* it—not propelling ourselves toward a more successful life, but rather getting out of the way of the good life that wants to live through us.

Richard Leider's purpose emerged over stages in his life. While in college, he was inspired by the work of leading psychologists such as Carl Rogers, Carl Jung, and Victor Frankl. In Frankl, he saw a teacher who lived what he taught with uncommon courage and conviction. Richard was later approached by a former priest who became a friend and mentor and had a lasting impact on his life by bringing a spiritual grounding to his work (the same former priest, incidentally, who wrote the seminal career-changing book *What Color Is Your Parachute?*—Richard Bolles). Finally, at Harvard he became involved with a project that was the largest study of adult development in the world. As Leider recalls, "I was introduced then to my life's work." He discovered that he wanted to take that kind of information and bring it into practice in the world, "living in the question of what's possible and the whole notion of 'calling.' This is what turned me on."

Together, these influences led him to his own purpose. From there, he wrote a series of books (including the best-selling *The Power of Purpose*) and developed a vocation in which he pursues his purpose every day, connecting with some of the world's most dynamic leaders in the process. Every year he also guides a group of leaders from around the world on an African excursion on the Serengeti Plain in East Africa, helping them discover their purpose and improve their leadership through a process of reflection, dialogue, and what he calls an "inventure expedition." That in turn gives him an opportunity to look deep within and reconnect with his own core identity.

AUTHENTIC INTEGRITY

Our values and purpose form our core identity—who we truly are, the expression of our true nature. If the first step on the path of the life entrepreneur is discovering core identity, the best way to take that first step is through what we call *authentic integrity*.

Without integrity, our lives and work are compromised. Integrity is the sine qua non of worthy endeavors and living. Most people think of integrity as steadfast adherence to a strict moral code, but it also entails integration of all aspects of our lives in a way that coheres. (The word is derived from *integer*, which means "whole" or "complete.") According to author Kevin Cashman, "Integrity goes far beyond telling the truth. Integrity means total congruence between who we are and what we do."

We would add that this congruence must be *authentic*—genuine and of true origin. "A happy life," said the Roman philosopher Seneca, "is one which is in accordance with its own nature." It may sound simple, but it is one of the most difficult things to achieve in practice because of all the countervailing pressures we encounter. Abraham Lincoln warned that "every man is born an original, but sadly most men die copies."

In our interview, musician Mary Cutrufello told us, "I've had people tell me I've lived a courageous life, but I don't particularly feel that way. I just felt like I've lived a life that was true to itself. . . . Anybody who's ever hung out in an 'old man bar'—you know what I'm talking about—sees what happens when you don't let that part of yourself do its thing." It's that kind of authentic integrity that drives her to be true to her muse even when the road is long and unforgiving.

Each of us must find a way to discover our core identity so we can be the author of our lives, even if the story line takes us in directions we never anticipated. Clearly articulating our history, current circumstances, relationships, needs, strengths, passions, values, and purpose is the first step on the entrepreneurial path—and a big leap forward in creating an extraordinary life. When we do, we become more attuned to previously unseen opportunities that resonate with our core identity but might otherwise pass by unnoticed.

See *www.lifeentrepreneurs.com* for exercises related to discovering core identity.

PART TWO

PREPARING FOR THE JOURNEY

CHAPTER FOUR

AWAKENING TO OPPORTUNITY

He who refuses to embrace a unique opportunity
loses the prize as surely as if he had failed.
—WILLIAM JAMES

Once we have a clearer sense of who we are and what we need and value, we become more awake to opportunities that may arise that resonate with what we want to do with our lives. Though there is a natural flow to this that sometimes clicks on its own, there is also a process that can help us take full advantage of the opportunities that arise. This includes opening up to possibility, recognizing opportunity, and then assessing it. Just as opportunity recognition is a cornerstone of business and social entrepreneurship, so it is with life entrepreneurship.

CAKE LOVE

Strolling into Cake Love, Warren Brown's bakery in the historic U Street district of Washington, D.C., you first encounter the alluring aroma of chocolate. The swirl of activity—puffs of flour, a ringing register, ovens popping open and shut, the line out the door—makes it a "scene," not just a bakery. In the center of it all is Warren, over six feet tall, with dreadlocks and a contagious grin. He was once named one of America's fifty most eligible bachelors by *People* magazine. But what is most remarkable is his obsession with baking. Warren is a nut about his sugary delicacies—about new recipes, his favorite flavors, even the chemistry behind each of his cakes—and it shows.

The success of Cake Love allowed him to open a coffee shop (the Love Café) across the street and later expand to more locations in neighboring Maryland and Virginia. Since then he has spread his wings as the host of a food show called *Sugar Rush* on the Food Network and dreamed up a new offering: a line of nutrition bars.

Warren is so much in his element that it is hard to imagine him doing anything else. But before Cake Love, Warren was a lawyer with the U.S. Department of Health and Human Services, struggling to find passion in his work. He had chosen law school, he says, because "I was driven by the expectation that I needed some type of profession. [I was also] driven by parental expectations and by looking at my peers."

Fresh out of law school, Warren got a message from the universe—at a Tibetan Freedom Festival, of all places. At the end of the Radiohead song "Karma Police," the lyrics cry out: "For a minute there I lost myself, I lost myself . . ." For Warren, these words hit deep. Feeling lost too, he started asking himself, Are you there? Are you happy? Are you ready? Are you *you*?

The questions rang in his head for months, so much so that Warren resolved to change his life. He started by conjuring a personal mantra: "Direct yourself to greatness, answer your call, and answer to yourself."

Returning to a lifelong passion, he started baking. He recalls that for the preceding year he "had been waiting for something to happen, and it never did. I was tired of waiting. It was time to make cake."

He enrolled himself in what he now jokingly calls the "Warren Brown School of Baking" and started experimenting. At first, his desserts were "terrible," but with practice he improved. Realizing he had tapped into a deep passion, he decided to announce to his family (an announcement made strategically over a home-made brunch) that he was considering leaving law and getting into the food business. They were immediately supportive. A month later, he took one of his dessert treats to family in upstate New York. When he walked through the airport carrying a chocolate cake, "Everyone had a response . . . more and more response," he recalls. "What I took away from it is that everyone wants to talk about cake. It always has a good association.

When I was waiting for my ride at the airport, it hit me: Go for the cakes. This is clearly something that people want. Make cake!"

Back home in D.C., he started scoping out bakeries in the area. "I was appalled by what people thought a bakery was," he says. "It was very different from what was in my head." To test his mettle as a cake baker, he transformed his kitchen into a cake lab and starting holding cake open houses, which led to a side business fulfilling cake orders. A few months later, gaining confidence and momentum, he walked into his law office and requested leave from his job.

The year that followed was full of challenges, but with every serious down there was also an up. For example, just before he ran out of cash, the local newspaper featured his story, and sales quadrupled overnight. Within the year, he submitted his formal resignation to the Department of Health and Human Services and fell into Cake Love.

WAKING UP TO POSSIBILITY

The real voyage of discovery consists not in seeking new lands, but in seeing with new eyes.
—MARCEL PROUST

Life entrepreneurs resolve to shape their own destiny. In doing so, they must be awake to possibility, recognizing that when we embrace big new ideas we can elevate our condition and help others to do the same. When we do, we often find ourselves, suddenly, in the right place at the right time, surrounded by the right people, thinking about the right things. Rather than being tossed about by changing circumstances, we discover opportunity in challenge and change.

Accepting the possibility of change often means overriding our psychological circuitry. In their paper, "The Neuroscience of Leadership," David Rock and Jeffrey Schwartz write, "Large-scale behavior change requires a large-scale change in mental maps." Human beings are wired to box things in. According to Dr. Edward De Bono, a leading international expert on human cognition, our thoughts become "etched" into our brains each time we think them, strengthening as electrical connections and making it harder for us to change.[1] Parents have expectations for us, teachers coach us into a particular mold, employers slot us into a defined job, and even our friends have expectations for us. We are unknowing coconspirators in this process, and the ruts of our routines grow deeper as we grow older, making it even harder to change the way we do things.

Psychologist Martin Seligman once sought to find out why it is so difficult for those who are depressed (but not clinically depressed—that is, in need of medical intervention) to change both their perception of life and their ability to do something about it. He discovered that they have a sense of "learned helplessness," believing that life is beyond their control and that setbacks are both permanent and their fault. As Seligman writes in *Learned Optimism,* "Learned helplessness is the giving up reaction, the quitting response that follows from the belief that whatever you do doesn't matter."[2]

Optimists, on the other hand, take life by the horns, intrinsically believing it is theirs to take. The pessimist's helplessness is replaced by hopefulness; quitting is replaced by persistence and tenacity. Optimists (and life entrepreneurs) are inclined to see opportunities where others see barriers.

Of course, optimists also experience setbacks, but their reaction to these setbacks sets them apart. The optimist sees a negative event as a temporary setback, something to be learned from, specific to that event, and a consequence of factors that often aren't her fault.[3] (Incidentally, optimists may live longer. A nine-year study of nearly a thousand men and women aged sixty-five to eighty-five found that highly optimistic people had a 55 percent lower risk of death from all causes and a 23 percent lower risk of death from heart failure than do strong pessimists.[4])

In her book *Mindset,* Stanford University professor Carol Dweck addresses what sets highly successful, creative people apart from people who struggle in life. In her research, which echoes Seligman's, she found that there are generally two different kinds of mind-sets: a "growth" mind-set and a "fixed" mind-set. The former is awake to possibility, embraces challenge, and takes risks ("nothing ventured, nothing gained"). The person with a fixed mind-set, in contrast, lives with a fear of failure and looking bad among his peers, and so seeks out a comfortable place where he can protect himself from embarrassing setbacks (a "nothing ventured, nothing lost" approach).[5]

Harvard University psychologist Ellen Langer also addresses these themes in her book *Mindfulness,* in which she distinguishes a "mindless" mental framework from a "mindful" one. The roots of mindless states are making "premature cognitive commitments," assuming linearity and limited resources, focusing exclusively on outcome and not on process, and rigidly relying on old categories. An example is the spouse who thinks of herself only in terms of her husband and children, without acknowledging her other relationships with relatives, friends, and neighbors or her other interests and skills that also carry great potential. Think of our limiting assumptions about old age and retirement—how we conflate old age with poor health and lack of mental and physical activity. As Langer writes, "Many of the limits we accept as real are illusory."[6]

By contrast, mindfulness entails continually creating new categories, remaining open to new information and different points of view, accepting uncertainty, changing the context, reframing, and enlisting the mind in creative and playful ways. In a state of mindfulness, we can become "switched on" to the opportunities around us.

"BEGINNER'S MIND"

In the beginner's mind there are many possibilities, but in the expert's there are few.
—SHUNRYU SUZUKI-ROSHI, SOTO ZEN PRIEST

Both of us have young daughters under the age of three. Watching them play is infectious—and instructive. Their play is a pure embodiment of exploration and wonder. For them, yogurt can be paint, glue, or hair gel as well as a yummy treat. A box presents a perfect opportunity to create a magical hiding place or a launching pad for a pint-sized superhero. Children are the natural proprietors of what Soto Zen priest Shunryu Suzuki-Roshi called "beginner's mind." This mind-set allows thoughts to fly about unencumbered by preconceptions. When they do, we see that the world is full of untapped opportunities. By contrast, the expert's mind is latched onto prior judgments and a fixed point of view, much like what Langer calls mindlessness.

As adults, we are often too "smart" for our own good. Pablo Picasso once observed that "all children are artists; the problem is how they remain artists when they grow up." When we cross into the land of adulthood, we start obsessing over all the ways things can go wrong. We talk ourselves out of a dream or a vision for a different future because of its complications and impracticalities. Too often, we miss out on opportunities because we confine ourselves to mental models of the world that are small and inhibited, bounding our own possibilities.

Peter Guber, chairman of Mandalay Entertainment, tells the story of *Gorillas in the Mist,* the acclaimed 1988 movie starring Sigourney Weaver that depicted the adventures of Dian Fossey as she studied and learned to communicate with the rare mountain gorillas of Africa. According to Guber, the film almost got shelved when it turned into a "logistical nightmare." The plan was to film using more than two hundred animals at an altitude of eleven thousand feet in Rwanda, a country that was then on the verge of a revolution. Warner Brothers was concerned that the filmmakers would exceed their budget, and the production plan required that the gorillas do what was scripted— essentially, to "act." If the team couldn't figure out a way to make that happen, they would have to go to plan B: "using dwarfs in gorilla suits on a soundstage."

In the middle of an emergency meeting, as Guber recounts, "A young intern asked, 'What if we let the gorillas write the story?' Everyone laughed and wondered what she was doing in a meeting with experienced filmmakers. Hours later, someone casually asked her what she had meant. She said, 'What if you sent a really good cinematographer into the jungle with a ton of film to shoot the gorillas? Then you could write a story around what the gorillas did on film.' It was a brilliant idea. And we did exactly as she suggested."

The result: they shot the film for half of the original budget, and the movie grossed more than $61 million worldwide. Guber was astonished at how the young intern's "'inexperience' enabled her to see opportunities where we saw only boundaries."[7]

When Cory Booker was working with youth in a classroom from a poor community in East Palo Alto, California, he asked the students to raise their hands as high as they could. He then challenged them to raise them a little higher, offering a prize to the one who could reach the highest. Suddenly a short, tough lad named Robert burst out of the room. Cory ran after him, ready to apologize for putting him in a no-win situation. Little Robert turned around and proclaimed, "I know a way to get to the roof!" Booker let him go up and win the prize, smiling at the boy's "beginner's mind."

Recognizing Opportunity

*All of us, whether or not we are warriors, have a
cubic centimeter of chance that pops out in front of
our eyes from time to time. The difference between
an average man and a warrior is that the warrior
is aware of this, and one of his tasks is to be
alert, deliberately waiting, so that when his cubic
centimeter pops out he has the necessary speed, the
prowess, to pick it up.*
—Carlos Castaneda, author

The "cubic centimeter of chance that pops out in front of our eyes" is opportunity calling. Recognizing it requires not only being alert but also being aware. That awareness must be both internal and external, giving us an intimate knowledge of our inner landscape of core identity and of our outer surroundings. Once we have that grounding, we can survey the landscape for opportunities. If we look closely, we are likely to find that opportunities are plentiful. The composer Johann Sebastian Bach, when asked how he found his melodies, is said to have replied, "The problem is not finding them, it's when getting up in the morning and getting out of bed, not stepping on them."

Natalie Kilassy is someone who has become adept at spotting opportunities, even in the unlikeliest of places. Living in a mining community in northeastern South Africa, she grew up in a family beset by hardship. When she was twenty-two, her father's business was liquidated, and the family was forced to take out steep loans to save their home. To help pay off the loans, Natalie and her new husband, Tim, started a small engraving company. That experience, she says, "made me fight. It was survival that made me come up with this passion and drive. I wanted to stand up for my life as a young girl and make a difference."

By the time she turned twenty-five, she was pregnant and still shouldering her family's debts. As she and Tim were surveying the landscape for new opportunities, they realized that the local miners were in need of higher-quality jackets, shoes, and protective equipment. So they recruited a business partner with sewing skills and created a company called Stitch Wise to meet those needs. "At the early stages," she recalls, "it was just an absolute need to take the risk and hope it works."

Two years later, Natalie spotted another opportunity: just behind her small office was a salvage yard with scraps of metal and old cabling from the mine. Every morning, men who had become severely disabled through mining accidents were put to work there, often in an alcoholic haze, stripping cable. The rates of depression were astronomical. She recalls thinking, "There's something I can do here. We can teach them how to sew. Give them something back in life."

Natalie approached the mine's executives and proposed a basic sewing skills course—to be funded by a new contract for rainwear that could be used to pay the men she would teach to sew. After winning the contract, she encountered a big problem: she was getting so squeezed by the mine on the cost of supplies and the price they were willing pay for the rainwear that the whole arrangement was becoming financially unsustainable. Rather than shut down the new program, Natalie pressed on. "You've got to keep going," she explains. "That's my nature, to just continuously fight and move on." Not only that, she decided to "shoot the moon," making a documentary about the program without the mine's knowledge. But instead of taking the mine to task about unfair pricing, she highlighted its willingness to educate and employ disabled miners.

When the documentary first aired on local television, the mine bosses were furious. But Natalie then received a call from the head of the mine's public relations department, who said, "What you did was wrong . . . but well done, it was a damn good story."

Shortly thereafter, Natalie managed to get a meeting with the mine manager and proposed designing and manufacturing a "backfill bag" that would make it both safer and easier for miners to extract gold. It would address the root cause of the astounding rate of disabilities caused by the mining and provide a new revenue source allowing her to employ injured miners. Impressed by her tenacity and ingenuity, the manager gave her access to his mines to begin the research and development process.

For the next eighteen months, Natalie put on a hard hat and spent countless hours underground pinpointing the safety problems and then testing various solutions. She eventually devised a highly effective (and patentable) solution. Within a few weeks, she landed her first order from the mine. Word soon began to spread through the international mining community.

Today, Stitch Wise provides more than 1,200 backfill bags a year to all of the gold-mining operations in South Africa and has branched into twelve new products, including selling 15,000 pairs of knee guards a month. The company now employs 166 people, 59 percent of whom are disabled, and offers basic education, adult literacy, business training, computer skills, and mentoring to its employees.

BREAKTHROUGH INNOVATION

> *I make more mistakes than anyone I know. And*
> *eventually I patent them.*
> —THOMAS EDISON

For life entrepreneurs, merely recognizing an opportunity or need is not enough. We need to be able to craft a solution that is compelling and timely and that breaks through the clutter of the status quo. We call this *breakthrough innovation*.

Many people use the terms *innovation* and *creativity* interchangeably, but there is an important distinction between them. Creativity typically refers to the act of producing new ideas, approaches, or actions. Innovation, by contrast, is the process of generating and *applying* such creativity in a specific context. Innovation can be thought of as the introduction of something new and useful, and it occurs when someone uses an invention— or deploys existing tools in new ways—to effect change.

According to Peter Drucker, innovation is at the heart of entrepreneurship: "Innovation is the specific tool of entrepreneurs, the means by which they exploit change as an opportunity for a different business or a different service. . . . [Entrepreneurs focus on] doing something different rather than doing better what is already being done . . ."[8]

The life entrepreneur searches for ways to change reality in powerful ways. Historically, breakthroughs often show up as paradigm shifts. Think Darwin, Einstein, plate tectonics, and quantum mechanics—all major upendings of prevailing worldviews. In the 1990s, Clayton Christensen of Harvard Business School coined the term *disruptive innovation*, which means overturning the dominant technology, product, service, or mode of operating in a market. Examples abound: the shift from sailboats to steam engines, horses to automobiles, mainframes to minicomputers, and record players to eight-tracks to cassette players to compact discs to digital audio players and so on. Even a pitcher's curveball can be thought of as a disruptive innovation (and according to baseball lore, the "skewball" was originally outlawed when it was introduced in the nineteenth century).

For the life entrepreneur, breakthrough innovation is a game changer that enables her to shatter the status quo by being willing to break a few rules—and lightbulbs—along the way.

BREAK ON THROUGH . . .

Richard Tait has been an entrepreneur since he was a young boy in Scotland. "Ever since the age of four," he says, "I've been creating businesses in my head. And I still do it all the time. . . . The greatest gift that my parents ever gave me was the freedom to dream."

Richard ended up coming to the United States for business school at the age of twenty-one and then headed off to Microsoft, becoming employee of the year in 1994 (at a time when Microsoft had thirty-five thousand employees). Richard thrived in Microsoft's hard-charging, entrepreneurial climate, eventually helping to start and run several new businesses, but after nine years, Microsoft's corporate culture had started to shift away from Richard's comfort zone. He started wondering if he could be a successful entrepreneur outside of Microsoft's cash-rich climate. It became a question that he couldn't shake. In his tenth year, he left. The only problem was that he had no plan for what was next—no idea whatsoever.

When he told his parents that he had left Microsoft, his dad asked, "What am I going to tell my friends?" Richard replied, "Tell them that your son is pursuing his heart." But inside Richard's head, things weren't so sanguine. "I had the equivalent of writer's block for entrepreneurs. Normally I have three new business ideas a day, but when I really needed it, nothing." It was 1998, the peak of the dot-com boom, and all of the ideas were swirling around the next big thing on the Web.

Nine long months later, he was playing games on a rainy day with his wife and another couple. He became frustrated that each of the games was so one-dimensional, with a winner-take-all mentality. As he pondered the problem, he had a breakthrough idea: develop a new kind of game that would give "everybody a chance to shine." And rather than create the game for the computer and exacerbate the societal isolation that he saw as a growing problem, Richard sought to create a board game that would bring people and families together in fun and engaging ways. "The insight," he says, "was just to rhyme human togetherness." In the next two weeks, Richard translated this vision into a twenty-two-page plan for a "lifestyles brand company." And thus was born Cranium, now the number-three brand in the game aisle.

But Cranium's success is not solely the result of a single breakthrough idea; rather, it can be attributed to ongoing opportunity recognition and a deep commitment to innovation. For example, when Richard and his business partner launched their company, both were new to the game industry and weren't aware of the fact that all retailers make their purchasing decisions in February—which was four months *before* their nascent company had twenty-seven thousand games en route in a truck with nowhere to be sold. Drowning their sorrows at a local Starbucks, Tait wondered to himself, *Why not take our games to where the customers are instead of where games are typically sold?* That innovative idea led to a pioneering distribution deal with Starbucks that put the new company solidly on the map.

In pursuit of game-changing innovation, Tait is adamant that the employees at Cranium have the license to take risks and fail. He says, "You have to tell people that taking risks is okay. . . . You have to let them know [they] can make mistakes. You have to allow people to learn."[9]

ASSESSING OPPORTUNITY

In retrospect, it is perhaps easy to see how Warren, Natalie, and Richard spotted a series of needs and their corresponding opportunities. But when opportunities first arise, the picture is often muddled. Typically, we are faced with several options and forced to make quick decisions in a context of uncertainty.

When Natalie's family was weighed down with debt and the small engraving company wasn't generating enough cash, there were many avenues she could have gone down. Her older brother headed south in search of a well-paying job. But Natalie and her husband took a chance on sewing handmade clothes for miners. Similarly, Warren left a stable government career and started a cake company in the face of long odds. As for Richard, people were bewildered when he started a board game company at the height of the internet boom. So why did these three make the decisions they did?

Often, the criteria we use to assess an opportunity are values based—for example, Natalie's decision to stay close to her family in a time of crisis and to focus her search locally. But we are also wise to evaluate an opportunity based on its objective potential, weighing it against other options and then deciding whether it is worth further exploration.

The opportunity assessment process is like a large funnel in which a number of ideas are pulled into the cone for consideration: some are interesting enough to be pulled further in for additional exploration, a few are thought through in detail, and only one comes out the other end—having made the transition from possibility to action. (Of course, we should refine our criteria as the stakes rise, such as when we are investing a large share of our savings or getting married.)

We must each develop our own process for assessing opportunities. Of the folks we interviewed, some relied entirely on their gut, while others were much more methodical. Sometimes the deliberation and decision were almost instantaneous; other times people eased into a decision after a painstaking process of advice gathering, analysis, and soul-searching.

Ultimately, though, we have to choose. Whatever the right combination of instinct versus research and analysis, we can't linger too long at the forks in the road. Making choices requires confronting trade-offs. Too many people get stuck, awash in options and awaiting that ever-elusive sign from above. Life entrepreneurship requires not only opening new doors but also walking through some and forgoing others. We have a limited capacity for pursuing new opportunities, especially big ones. If we try to chase down every opportunity that comes our way, we inhibit our ability to pounce on the promising ones that fit with our values and direction. According to Barry Schwartz, author of *The Paradox of Choice: Why More Is Less:*

> Every choice we make is a testament to our autonomy, to our sense of self-determination. . . . And each new expansion of choice gives us another opportunity to assert our autonomy, and thus display our character. . . . To avoid the escalation of such burdens (too many choices), we must learn to be selective in exercising our choices. We must decide, individually, when choice really matters and focus our energies there, even if it means letting many other opportunities pass us by. The choice of when to be a chooser may be the most important choice we have to make.[10]

In the end, life entrepreneurs must recognize (or create) opportunities and choose, proactively and purposefully, which ones to seize.

"YOUR LIFE IS YOUR ART"

And the day came when the risk to remain tight in the bud was more painful than the risk it took to blossom.
—ANAIS NIN

When she was in her twenties, Kimberly Wilson had to decide which opportunities to seize. She had grown up in Lawton,

Oklahoma, and became smitten with dancing, especially ballet. After graduate school, she backpacked through Europe and took a year off to "ski and play" in Colorado. Then she drifted a bit in her own intense way, as only a self-described "type A" personality can do—working in retail, pursuing a degree in paralegal studies, working at a law firm, then serving as executive assistant to a paralegal program. Exhausted, she took up yoga to handle the stress and was immediately drawn to its elegant combination of fitness, harmony, health, and balance.

One day, she awakened to the possibility of becoming a yoga instructor. Minimizing the financial risk and keeping her options open, she opened a yoga "studio" in her living room while maintaining her job. Before she knew it, she found herself teaching ten classes a week on top of her forty to fifty-hour workweeks. When she returned from a two-week yoga teacher training session, she knew she was at a crossroads: "When I came back to my job," she remembers, "I cried. I realized this is not me. I was working to get paid and for the health benefits, but I was killing my soul. . . . I felt torn. It wasn't the direction I wanted to be going. So I quit."

It wasn't just possibility she saw in front of her. She also spotted a need. She had observed lots of young professionals from other states who were now living in the nation's capital and, like her, yearning for authentic connections with others and a sense of community that also fit with their active lifestyle. By creatively addressing those identified needs, she was able to compose in her imagination a vision of a warm and thriving community-based yoga studio that healed stressed-out bodies and nurtured lonely souls. Embedded in that vision was a new life for her that fit with who she wanted to become.

All that was left was to seize the opportunity before her. Her newfound freedom to pursue her dream was both intoxicating and scary. "I was kind of panic-stricken," she recalls, "with emotions ranging from being terrified about what I am doing to total excitement. . . . It was this mix of exhilaration, excitement, and fear of the unknown."

Today, she leads a hip yoga enterprise in D.C., with two yoga studios (named Tranquil Space) serving about 650 people each week and a nascent foundation focused on mentoring disadvantaged girls. She runs the business and the foundation and has written a book, *Hip Tranquil Chick: A Guide to Life On and Off the Yoga Mat*. She also gets to do what she loves every day: building a community of people who share similar values and interests—and even designing a yoga clothing line.

She adds that starting her own business was "a huge reflection of becoming more self-confident. . . . It is very empowering to feel like I could create my own reality." What does she tell the young women she mentors? "Chart your own course! You have to wake up every day with yourself . . . [Y]our life is your art, and I am constantly working to create mine. My business is my passion. . . . I get so excited talking about it and helping women realize that you can leave a loveless full-time job and create the life you desire."[11]

Creating the life we desire starts with awakening to possibility. Seeing with "new eyes," we can recognize and assess opportunities and then seize them. Like Kimberly, we start by folding them into a vision for what our life can be.

CHAPTER FIVE

ENVISIONING THE FUTURE

We are what we imagine ourselves to be.
—KURT VONNEGUT

In the early 1900s, a young mechanic from a Michigan farm had a vision:

> I will build a motor car for the great multitude. . . . It will be so low
> in price that no man making a good salary will be unable to own
> one and enjoy with his family the blessings of hours of pleasure in
> God's great open spaces. . . . When I'm through, everybody will be
> able to afford one, and everyone will have one. The horse will have
> disappeared from our highways, the automobile will be taken for
> granted . . . [and we will] give a large number of men employment
> at good wages.[1]

At the time, Americans owned only eight thousand cars and the country had a paltry 144 miles of paved roads; Henry Ford was coming off of a failed company and an altercation with investors. The picture he painted then was nearly unimaginable. Today, the United States has 243 million cars and four million miles of paved roads,[2] and Ford Motor Company is a $160 billion company with more than three hundred thousand employees worldwide—a tangible tribute to the power of one man's vision.

For Murem Sharpe, the vision for her start-up company was inspired by events closer to home. Her father had recently passed away, and she regretted that her family had never captured his voice and stories for future generations to hear. She was also struck by the gut-wrenching stories of victims of the September 11 attacks, whose final thoughts to their loved ones from United flight 93 and the twin towers were captured on voice mail.

Together, these events inspired her to create a way to record and share voice recordings easily, using telephone, internet, and MP3 technology. So the former corporate executive and mother of two grown children partnered with a tech-savvy twenty-something named Diego Orjuela and launched Evoca, an internet-enabled voice recording company, with the following vision: "Evoca will change the way we communicate by empowering voices in ways never imagined before. We envision people everywhere speaking their minds, sharing their ideas, and storing their memories on Evoca. We see voice becoming the next tool for publishing and communicating online and through your telephone."[3]

Today, that vision is coming to fruition: students from Turkey are using Evoca to put voice recordings on their internet profiles; Rafael Korcya, the president of Ecuador, uses it to post recordings to his website; and U.S. presidential candidates are using the service to reach voters.[4]

A gravelly recording of one of the most enduring examples of an inspiring vision has been heard by three generations of schoolchildren. Spoken on the steps of the Lincoln Memorial in August 1963, it still inspires:

> I have a dream that one day this nation will rise up and live out the true meaning of its creed: "We hold these truths to be self-evident; that all men are created equal." I have a dream that one day on the red hills of Georgia the sons of former slaves and the sons of former slave owners will be able to sit down together at the table of brotherhood. . . . I have a dream that my four little children will one day live in a nation where they will not be judged by the color of their skin but by the content of their character. . . . With this faith we will be able to transform the jangling discords of our nation into a beautiful symphony of brotherhood.[5]

When Martin Luther King Jr. pronounced his vision, he challenged us to take part in bringing it to fruition. He summoned us to relinquish a troubled past with full faith in better days ahead.

A vision is a bold and vivid picture of a better future. It should inform as well as inspire, calling on us to imagine and participate in that future. Applying this to our lives, a vision should clearly describe where we want to go.[6] A well-designed vision paints a picture of our desired destination across all the important aspects of our lives. Aristotle observed that "the soul never thinks without a picture." Our life vision should take our breath away with its audacity, roaring with passion and setting a marker for what we plan to do with our days on the planet.

In this chapter, we discuss the creation of a strong vision statement and show how vision has evolved for a number of life entrepreneurs.

CREATING A VISION FOR OUR LIVES

Many organizations craft a banner vision statement to inspire their efforts toward success, but most people haven't thought to do so for themselves. For life entrepreneurs, translating our core identity into a vision for our life points us in the direction that we aim to go in the future.

As we craft a vision for our lives, we should ensure that it is

- Vivid in its description
- Unbounded by the status quo
- Aligned with our core identity
- Distant enough that we have to work toward it
- Clear enough that we can measure our progress against it
- Broad enough to encompass all the major aspects of our lives (including personal, professional, and relationships) (see Figure 5.1)

Developing a vision is an exercise in thinking big and long term—not in setting next year's resolutions. The best time frame to use is ten years or more—even an entire lifetime—long enough for us to be able to set a very high bar while also giving us enough time to hurdle it.

A vision should also be specific enough to mean something—and clear enough to lead naturally to specific goals and strategies. We must be able to gauge progress against our vision.

FIGURE 5.1.   CATEGORIES FOR LIFE'S VISIONS.

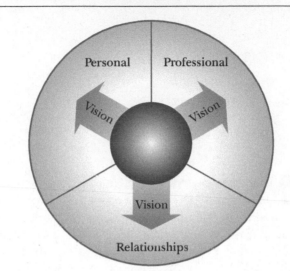

Though specific, a vision should not be prescriptive. Ford's vision entailed making a car so affordable that anyone could experience the joy of a road trip, but he didn't mention anything about an assembly line or Model T. A good vision is directional but not tactical, not interloping into issues of process—of *how* we will get there (which is the province of strategy and tactics). By keeping our vision open, we can work on achieving it from a variety of angles. A vision statement should be roughly a paragraph or two in length, no more than a page, and written in the present tense as if that vision were being accomplished.

Example of a Personal Vision Statement

[In ten years . . .] I am an accomplished artist with several solo shows to my name. I have traveled the world extensively, learning about new cultures that have in turn been represented in my paintings. Through my work and studio, I am able to make a direct contribution to my community—through both my civic leadership and my commitment to teaching art to young people. I am deeply committed and connected to my family and friends and maintain an active and healthy lifestyle. I live in a place that stimulates my creativity daily and continues to introduce me to new and exciting people.

Further examples and exercises on creating a personal vision statement can be found on this book's website: www.lifeentrepreneurs.com.

IMAGINING THE FUTURE

We think about the future in a way that no other animal can, does, or ever has, and this simple, ubiquitous, ordinary act is a defining feature of our humanity.
—DANIEL GILBERT[7]

If thinking about the future is a defining feature of our humanity, as Harvard University professor Daniel Gilbert posits, it is the fertile use of our imagination that often takes us to transcendent heights. What would our world be like without the visionaries who have brought their dreams to life in service of new products, engaging entertainment, social movements, and a better quality of life?

In imagining the future, though, we rapidly run into a daunting stumbling block. As Gilbert writes, our "imagination cannot easily transcend the boundaries of the present."[8] To prove his point, he offers a number of humorous and telling examples. For instance, in 1899 the commissioner of the U.S. Office of Patents declared that "everything that can be invented has been invented."[9] Not long before the Wright brothers took flight at Kitty Hawk, renowned physicist Lord William Kelvin concluded that "heavier-than-air flying machines are impossible."

The problem, Gilbert points out, is that we humans are constrained by "presentism": "Most of us have a tough time imagining a tomorrow that is terribly different from today."[10] This presents a recurring problem in our institutions and society, as our leaders and policymakers often resort to solutions that only nibble around the edges of change.

Imagining a different future requires changing our mental frameworks. Famed mountaineer Reinhold Messner thinks of it as "probing the edges of what might be possible." Sometimes that means not taking no for an answer, pushing beyond the limits, or refusing to be confined by present circumstance.

Leila Velez knows something about imagining a different future. She was born in the 1970s in Rio de Janeiro, the daughter of a janitor who emigrated to Brazil with no money to try to start a better life. At ten, she got her first job delivering the clothes her mother, a laundry woman, washed to supplement her family's income. At fourteen, she went to work at McDonald's, "the only company that would hire me so young," she explains. She worked all day and attended school at night. She was fascinated by the McDonald's processes, quality controls, and obsessive focus on customer service. At sixteen, she became the youngest manager in Rio.

She met a boy named Rogerio in high school, fell in love, and later got married. Then, spotting opportunity, she started a business with his sister, Zica, who was a hairdresser. The inspiration for the business, it turns out, was kinky hair. Leila explains, "The hair was a problem. Having curly hair was a problem because we wanted to look more feminine, but our hair would grow up and out the sides."

Leila and Zica spent their free time experimenting with different products and raw materials to search for a solution to the problem. Rogerio was the primary guinea pig for their home-grown experiments: "He went bald a couple times because the mixture was really a mess," Leila recalls. "We had no idea what we were doing." They stuck with it until they finally created a formula that made their hair "well defined, with longer curls and no frizz. It was like a miracle," proclaims Leila.

Presciently, they hired a chemist to file a patent for the formula. Next, they opened a salon with money they raised from selling their beat-up Volkswagen Beetle and their life savings—the equivalent of US$3,000, all told. It was enough to rent a house that they could refurbish into a salon. Though they had no funds for advertising, their product was a big hit, leading to lots of buzz in the community—and referrals. Soon "the lines became bigger and bigger. We had to open earlier and close later." They opened a second salon, then a third.

As their budding enterprise grew, they wanted to offer new products and services but were disappointed with the quality of products from their suppliers. Desperate, they decided to open their own factory that would produce their own line of products.

Today, still in her early thirties, Leila is overseeing a budding empire of beauty products: Beleza Natural has six salons, 670 employees (70 percent of whom are former customers), and a cosmetics factory. Its growth shows no sign of slowing. In fact, in the coming year they plan to open three more salons. This has inspired Leila and Zica to create a bold vision for the future. "We dream big dreams," says Leila. "It takes the same amount of effort to dream small or dream big." First, she wants to conquer Brazil. "And then the whole world. Why not? We have six salons now and we always think about six hundred. Why not six thousand? I couldn't imagine only one salon. It was just the beginning." Today, she has her eye on Sao Paolo, Paris, and New York.

This janitor's daughter from humble beginnings clearly has refused to be constrained by "presentism," in business or in life. She also has visions and goals beyond Beleza Natural. One day, she hopes to become a teacher so she can encourage other people to follow their dreams and think big. But even as she thinks big, she recognizes the importance of "being humble and keeping our feet on the floor. . . . Sometimes success can be deceiving. If you feel that you have the key for everything and the answer for all the questions, I think that's the day when things become bad. I hope to keep my life in this continuous search."

AN EVOLVING VISION

Like Leila, many of the entrepreneurs we talked with had evolving visions for the future—both for themselves and their organizations. With time and experience, they gained clarity about where they wanted to go, but only after their vision had evolved considerably over time. Often, they found that their current enterprises and life path didn't reflect what was initially anticipated. As their aspirations, needs, and circumstances evolved, so did their visions.

Steve Ells, founder of the hugely successful Chipotle restaurant chain, took a meandering path through the first chapters of his life. As he admits, "I went from college graduation not having any idea what I was going to do, to cooking school not knowing that I was going to get into this restaurant business, to all of a sudden having a dream that, yeah, maybe I would like to be a chef restaurant owner, to all of a sudden running a restaurant chain."

Steve's vision has evolved from running a burrito joint in order to fund a gourmet restaurant to changing the world one burrito at a time. A few years ago, he was outraged to learn about the unconscionable conditions for the vast majority of livestock in the United States. Learning about the "dark side of agriculture" inspired him to do things differently. Today Chipotle's manifesto is "no less ambitious than revolutionizing the way America grows, gathers, serves, and eats its food."[11] Its "Food with Integrity" program has made Chipotle the largest restaurant seller of naturally raised meat in the world. The company now has more than six hundred restaurants across the country and earns over $500 million in revenue—quite a burrito joint.

This leads to an important insight about life entrepreneurship: the path is full of surprises. We seldom have the luxury of waiting until everything is crystal clear before getting started. However, our conversations with entrepreneurs like Leila and Steve revealed the importance of a clear vision in guiding our decisions, even if it may evolve over time.

CONNECTING VISION TO CORE IDENTITY

One of the essential points about vision is that our articulation of where we want to go needs to be grounded in who we are. Yet many people stumble on this step, neglecting to look inward before projecting outward. In essence, our vision statement is an authentic rendering of how our purpose and values can play out in the world. A personal vision statement asks: What do we want to be, do, and contribute in life? Our core identity helps us answer that question. As we have seen, discovering our core identity can be a long and involved process that takes time to ferment. And so it is sometimes with vision—especially one that truly connects to our core identity.

Take, for example, Gun Denhart, cofounder of the popular children's clothing line Hanna Andersson. The company is widely respected for being a socially responsible business, in large part due to her values, which evolved as her business evolved.

Her Swedish background, sense of social justice, and personal values all contributed to building a company whose vision transcends selling quality children's clothes. Hanna Andersson has given away over a million items of clothing and a percentage of its profits every year to non-profits serving vulnerable children.

Hanna Andersson's charitable giving program emerged out of Denhart's personal experience. When she first donated clothing to a local women's shelter, she caught her first glimpse of the needs in her local community. She recalls, "I can still remember the feeling I had when I realized, oh my God, there are children in America who don't have clothes. That hit me a lot . . . and changed how I looked at the business and at what I wanted to do in my life."

Based on these experiences and ongoing personal development, her vision for her life has also evolved, motivating Denhart to become a leading community and child advocate in her adopted hometown of Portland, Oregon. She also coauthored a book, *Growing Local Value: How to Build Business Partnerships That Strengthen Your Community,* and has since become an internationally prominent advocate of socially responsible business. As she shares her vision for a more sustainable future with audiences, it is clear that her vision for her life and work are merging— increasing the power of the message and the likelihood of it becoming a reality.

STAYING TRUE TO OUR VISION

Having a vision can be a catalyzing force in our lives, but we shouldn't expect that we will travel a linear path from point A to point B to realize it. Sometimes "stuff" happens. Our circumstances change. But life entrepreneurs hold fast to that vision and figure out a way to bring it to life.

The grandson of Ellis Island immigrants and the product of a working-class neighborhood in Lowell, Massachusetts, Gerald Chertavian grew up with a strong work ethic and a passion for serving others. Right after college graduation, he had become a Big Brother to a young boy from the Dominican Republic. "What I saw through David's eyes," he says, "was a world where he didn't know how to get in. I realized that we were wasting a lot of human capital in a country where we couldn't afford to waste it."

In his application to business school, Gerald wrote an impassioned essay about the need to teach basic business skills to low-income youth. It was a vision firmly grounded in his passions and values, but the excitement of it receded into the background behind the bombardment of daily priorities and competing claims.

Gerald graduated from business school and ended up moving to London to be with his fiancée. Following a frustrating job experience, he was approached by his tennis partner with an opportunity to buy into a technology company on the verge of bankruptcy. He had precious little to go on, save for an interest in the tech sector, but he decided to do it, even though it required that he take a pay cut and tap into his wife's savings to participate in the acquisition. With good timing and buckets of elbow grease, Gerald and his team built Conduit Communications into one of Britain's fastest-growing companies. Six years later they sold it for a significant return and made millionaires out of many of their colleagues in the process.

After the company was sold, Gerald phased out of the new company, opening a window of opportunity in his life. Through a process of reflection and advice gathering from his mentors, he decided it was time to make good on that business school essay and start an organization teaching business skills to underserved youth. It occurred to him, *I can do this.*

He then developed a business plan for Year Up, an intensive yearlong program that trains urban young adults and places them in the workplace. He says that the decision to start Year Up "was easy. . . . It's the most consistent decision I have ever made in terms of lining up what I am truly good at and what I am absolutely passionate about."

Gerald took a circuitous route in realizing his early vision, but his lucrative detours were full of experience gathering and learning that in turn enabled him to build Year Up into a nationally recognized, award-winning organization. Though his initial vision had been put on the shelf for a while, he didn't give up on it. He is now working to make sure the young people in Year Up are able to realize their vision too.

Many of us take a winding path in realizing our vision. The question is, will we return to it after wandering astray—and can we stick with it when times are tough?

The Power of Shared Vision

Despite the myth of the heroic visionary leader, there is little about developing and pursuing a vision that should be a solo endeavor. Life entrepreneurs recognize the power of a vision shared with the people in our lives: our spouses, friends, colleagues, and crew.

Howard Schultz is no exception. As we walk into the warm comfort of Starbucks for our morning pick-me-up, it is hard to imagine that the man who built it into an empire the size of a small country grew up in a public housing project in Brooklyn in a working-class family stretched to its limit. As a child, Howard recalls seeing his father "bitter as a result of being disrespected in the workplace as a blue-collar, uneducated worker."

One day when Howard was seven, he came home to find his father in a full-leg cast. He had slipped on the ice and broken his ankle—and lost his job and health benefits as a result. Howard was put in charge of answering the phone when the creditors called, to tell them his parents weren't home.

Still, his mom would tell him again and again, "You can be anything you want to be. You're going to be the first person in our family to graduate from college." And so he was—attending Michigan State on a football scholarship. But the starkness of his childhood carried forward: "I had a fear of failure and not getting out of that environment, which propelled me to want to overachieve."

After college, he worked for Xerox. He was making good money at a respectable company, living in the Village in New York, feeling "I have arrived." But eventually, being a small cog in a large bureaucratic empire wore on him. It wasn't long before he realized, "This is not me."

Around that time, he learned about an opportunity with a Swedish company called Hammerplast that was building a U.S. business. "A month later," he says, "I was in Sweden, training. I didn't know where I was going to land. It was like jumping off the cliff without a net, but I was fine with that. If you want to be an entrepreneur, one of the great questions you have to ask yourself is whether you have the courage to fail."

His travels for Hammerplast took him to Seattle, where "a company that no one had ever heard of called Starbucks was buying more than anyone [from suppliers]. I'd never been out here. I called my wife, Sheri, and said, 'You can't believe this place. It's so beautiful. The sun's out. I can see the mountains. People are sailing.' I then walked into Pike Place Market, felt the energy, walked into that store, smelled the coffee, had my first French press of Sumatra coffee. . . . I became so smitten with Seattle and Starbucks and I just felt, *this is me.* I told Sheri, 'We've got to live here. This is the place for us.'"

Howard tried for a year to convince the founders of Starbucks to hire him. They turned him down at first, but then reconsidered and hired him to head up the marketing department. "Then I go to Italy," he adds, "which is the real epiphany." He was enamored with the Italian espresso bars and wanted to re-create the barista magic in the United States, but Starbucks once again shot him down. It took him a year and a half to convince them to allow him to incorporate that idea into a new store. When he proposed an expansion, they turned him down again. Finally, he left Starbucks with their blessing to try to raise equity to bring his vision to life. That is when he stumbled upon a crossroads in his life:

> Nobody would give me the money. That's the year where I didn't have a salary and Sheri was pregnant with our first child. It was brutal. *Brutal.* Sheri's father comes to Seattle, I'll never forget this, and says, "I want to take a walk with you." He sits down on a park bench and says, "I want to be respectful. I know how hard you've worked, but my daughter is eight months pregnant. She's working. You're working with no salary. You need to give up this hobby and get a job." I just started crying, I was so embarrassed. I remember walking back to the house and I had to wipe my face when we got into the house. I told Sheri the story that night and if she would have said, "He's right," it would have been over. She was the one who said, "No way, we're going to do this." She was the one. . . . That was the turning point in our life that night. She never flinched.

Shortly thereafter, Howard closed the financing and launched a barista-style coffee shop called Il Giornale. It did well, and eventually they negotiated a deal to buy Starbucks, which was struggling with debt, for $3.8 million if they could find equity to cover it.

At the time, Starbucks had six retail stores. In the midst of this, one of Howard's investors tried to steal the deal out from under them. Howard asked Bill Gates Sr., father of the founder of Microsoft, to help and was able to stave off the defection—another near miss.

Howard is emphatic about the importance of all the people in his life, from family and friends to business associates. "I think the athletic experience that I've had—understanding what it means to be part of a team, self-sacrifice, sharing the stage, making others look good, and what it means to lock your arms together and defend together—has served me so well because so much about entrepreneurship is team building. . . . And you've got to have someone at home who believes in you and is willing to allow you to lean on them. . . . My wife, I just couldn't have done this without her."

This speaks to a broader cultural trend that Starbucks has tapped into: "Starbucks is the quintessential people-based business, where everything we do is about humanity. The culture and values of the company are its signature and its competitive difference. We have created a worldwide appeal for our customers because people are hungry for human connection and authenticity."[12] He continues, "I think people generally want to be part of something larger than themselves, but only if what they are looking at has a set of values and guiding principles that is compatible with their own."

Today, Starbucks is a socially conscious global enterprise that sells $8 billion worth of coffee each year from about thirteen thousand stores worldwide.[13] It is also creating pockets of community in all sorts of unexpected places. The vision of the life entrepreneur can be powerful beyond our wildest imagination—especially when it is a shared vision.

> *We are all angels with only one wing: we can only*
> *fly by embracing each other.*
> —LUCIANO DE CRESCENZO

Chapter Six

Developing Goals and Strategies

Coming out of college, Rob Glaser was fascinated with the intersection of media, communications, and technology. Two summers earlier, he had taken an internship with IBM. That was the summer, as it happened, that IBM launched the world's first personal computer (PC), giving Rob a front-row seat at the dawn of a new era in technology.

Believing that the PC was a remarkable and revolutionary product that would be central to the convergence of technology, media, and communications, he set a goal of working with a company that was well positioned, and he strategically evaluated job opportunities at several organizations with that goal in mind. He knew he didn't want to return to IBM, reasoning that it was too bureaucratic. Hewlett-Packard, although decentralized, was also too big and not at the forefront of the PC world. He considered an opportunity with a start-up in Stamford, Connecticut, designing personal finance software, but "I didn't really want to live there," he recalls, "and I wasn't passionate about that product." With his eclectic set of interests, from politics and economics to math, computers, and new media, he says, "I was interested in what I could do to synthesize all those things together."

The option that stood out was a rapidly growing software start-up in Bellevue, Washington, where everyone was "super smart and very passionate about what they did," he says.

Microsoft.

Rob was twenty-one at the time, and Bill Gates and Steve Ballmer were both twenty-eight. "I knew enough from my PC experience," Rob recalls, "to know that Microsoft had the operating system for the PC. . . . I was very impressed and I thought, *I'll do this until it gets boring and then maybe I'll start up my own thing.* . . . To my surprise and delight, it went from being $50 million in revenue to $4 billion when I left, and from about 250 people to closing on 10,000 when I left. It was a phenomenal ten-year ride."

After a series of rapid promotions, he was offered the chance to run a division that generated one-fifth of Microsoft's total revenue. He turned it down because it didn't fit with his life vision. "I passed on it," he says, "because it would have taken me further off the path of where I wanted to go." It was then that he realized, *I want to do something transcendent.*

With an emerging sense of where he wanted to go and a host of ideas for "the next big thing" in high tech, he decided he needed a strategy for how to approach his next steps. He took a six-month leave of absence in the summer of 1993 and went to Germany, Greece, and Egypt, determined to think through his options. He even developed his own personal decision-making matrix to help him analyze those options.

Just before he left, his friend Mitch Kapor, founder of Lotus, gave him some sage advice. Rob recounts, "He told me, 'Make sure that when you jump into something next, you have figured out not just what you want to do, but why you want to do it, because once it gets going, you're not going to have enough time to stop and contemplate.' That was very influential for me—to not just jump into the first thing that seemed mildly interesting out of fear of not doing anything."

When he returned, Rob decided to investigate how the emerging Internet might develop as a medium. He took two consulting jobs at Microsoft that allowed him to do just that, positioning himself to make an informed decision. After intensive strategic analysis, he narrowed his focus to two ideas with possible commercial appeal and eventually chose one.

In February 1994, he incorporated Progressive Networks (later to be renamed RealNetworks). His methodical planning process paid off. Within two years of launch, RealPlayer, the company's flagship product, became the dominant software for music and video in the burgeoning internet marketplace.

His vision of doing something transcendent was coming to fruition, but it had required adjusting his goals and strategy along the way. When the internet bubble burst in 2000, for instance, Rob and his RealNetworks team quickly shifted their strategy after a hardheaded assessment of their strengths and vulnerabilities. "We saw it coming," he says, "and we pivoted our company rapidly to focus more on our consumer businesses." Within four years, the company's revenue went from 70 percent business generated to 70 percent consumer generated, and they have since tripled their sales to almost $600 million.

As Rob's story illustrates, it is not enough to have big ideas and hope they come together. Once we have a good sense of where we want to go, we must articulate what we hope to accomplish (our goals) and then develop a plan for how to get there (our strategy). In this chapter, we address these concepts in turn.

Setting Goals

Goals are aims. They are the ends that we seek, the objectives we want to accomplish. Most people are familiar with setting and pursuing goals, but too few are acquainted with the essential characteristics of effective goals. With well-designed goals, we are more focused and accountable and, consequently, tend to achieve more. Effective goals are

- Purposeful and prioritized
- Clear and measurable
- Challenging but achievable

Purposeful and Prioritized

Goals are most effective when they are aligned with our purpose, values, and vision, emanating from them as a river flows from its source. When goals are aligned that way, they are naturally motivating. We must ensure that goals, if achieved, will lead us where we want to go. It is essential to be clear about the *why* behind our goals: Why do we want to achieve that goal? What benefits will occur if the goal is attained? Many emerging leaders, for example, started their careers with burning ambition and a goal of "running something." Only later do they see that this is not enough. *Why* do we want to run something? To what end?

Many entrepreneurs reason that their goal in starting a new venture is to achieve independence and control their own destiny. According to Amar Bhide, Columbia professor of entrepreneurship, those goals are too vague. What they really want, he reasons, is a chance to revel in developing new technology, an outlet for their artistic talent, or the opportunity to create something lasting that embodies their values.[1] Additional clarity can often be found by digging deeper, by continuing to ask the *why* question until it can be asked no more.

Effective goals should also be prioritized, helping us to weed out lower-priority activities that can impede us from accomplishing the things that really matter. As we set goals, we must continually ask: Is this goal truly a priority right now? What is the "opportunity cost"—the cost of the time and energy that could be spent on other pursuits—and is it worth it? Prioritization is important because sometimes goals are in conflict. The priority tells us which goal gets the nod when we are forced to make a difficult trade-off.

CLEAR AND MEASURABLE

Goals often suffer from a lack of clarity and specificity, usually due to a lack of time or attention in the goal-setting process. By making goals clear and specific, we increase our accountability. And the clearer we are about the required results, the more motivated we become to achieve them.

When Larry Leith first decided to start a restaurant, he had only a vague concept. He envisioned a restaurant that would serve healthy, good, and affordable Japanese food in a cool and fun atmosphere, playing hip new music in a space defined by its funky architecture. But what outcome was he truly hoping for? Finally, it became clear to him: he wanted to create an authentic restaurant that took care of its customers and its employees and became part of their lifestyle. He does that and more at Tokyo Joe's. "We call it the MoJoe," he quips, "and it's really important to us.

In everything we do, we're very clear about who we want to be and how we want to do it." This, in turn, has led to clear goals that pertain to different aspects of the business, from revenue and profit growth to employee retention to customer satisfaction and repeat-business rates.

For goals to carry any weight, they must also be measurable. We must know it when we have achieved them. For goals to be measurable, they must be time-bound. Without a clear deadline, goals have no "teeth." This is where many people miss the boat. It is one thing to aspire to launch a summer camp focused on leadership and life skills for disadvantaged youth, but until we add "within the next eighteen months" it's just pie in the sky. Max Israel, whom we met in Chapter One, set a personal goal of qualifying for the world Ironman triathlon championship in Hawaii within three years. In 2007, the KIPP network, which started as a small program in a Texas fifth-grade classroom in 1994, announced a goal of serving twenty-one thousand students in Houston through a cluster of forty-two schools within ten years. If every outcome that we strive for is that clear and measurable, we can then gauge our progress to see how far up the mountain we have climbed. What's more, our odds of achieving the goal increase dramatically.

Challenging but Achievable

Effective goals arise out of a healthy ambition to reach new heights. It is better to set our goals high and fail a few times than to rig the system with goals that are a walk in the park. Robert F. Kennedy reminds us that "only those who dare to fail miserably can achieve greatly." We should be careful not to confine ourselves, limiting our goals to our current station in life. In setting goals, we must leave room for the person we could become.

Billy Shore of Share Our Strength says, "I'm very comfortable setting goals that cannot necessarily be reached but that will inspire. . . . I don't feel bad if I don't meet them if they've actually helped me get farther than I otherwise would have gone." After reflecting on what he wanted to do with his life, Emmet Keeffe III, CEO and cofounder of software company iRise, set what he calls a "unique and crazy" goal: starting a Formula One (car racing) team. Having been a car racing fanatic as a boy, he explains, "I wanted to set a goal that I knew would make me happy." It was a classic example of a "BHAG"—a big, hairy, audacious goal.[2]

When Suzanne McKechnie Klahr was seventeen, she set an audacious goal for herself: improving the lives of a hundred thousand people through her work. Even in her idealistic, adolescent "I can do anything" state, she felt this notion was so out of bounds that she didn't dare utter it to anyone until she was twenty.

Coming out of law school, she turned down a prestigious position at a top law firm in New York City, raising eyebrows among her friends. She had recently been teaching low-income adults and students in East Palo Alto, California, how to start and run businesses, and she won a fellowship to continue that work. The experience directly connected with her passions, values, and sense of purpose and motivated her to launch a non-profit organization called BUILD, which helps underserved high school students start their own businesses. Her goals for BUILD are multifaceted: reaching students with potential but no motivation; breaking the vicious cycle of socioeconomic disadvantage; and empowering at-risk students to stretch themselves, gain confidence, attend college, and serve their communities as role models and leaders. For each goal, they develop metrics to show whether they are achieving them: percentage of students attending college, percentage of students engaging in community service, and more.

BUILD now provides entrepreneurial training and emotional support to more than three hundred disadvantaged students in eight schools in the San Francisco Bay Area and is planning to expand to the east coast. Her fifty alums have all enrolled in college (a distinctly different record from most of their peers).

When Suzanne was selected as an Ashoka fellow (Ashoka is an internationally recognized program promoting social entrepreneurship), her husband reminded her of the audacious goal that she had confided in him when they were dating in college. "If you keep up this rate of growth," he said, "in eight years you will have touched the lives of a hundred thousand people."

Like Emmet and Suzanne, we should be sure to set one or two BHAGs that are a monumental stretch. But we should also set goals that are both challenging and achievable in the short term, so we can methodically make tangible progress toward them—as Suzanne has done in subsequently setting a number of nearer-term goals that build toward her grander aspirations.

Common Stumbling Blocks

Despite our best attempts at setting effective goals, sometimes we fall short in the attempt. Here are the most common stumbling blocks in goal setting (and in striving to achieve them):

- *Setting the wrong goals.* We may mistakenly adopt someone else's goals, the goals we think we should have, or goals that others will admire or appreciate.
- *Having too many goals.* Having three to five well-constructed goals is much better than a litany of twenty goals that distract us from our priorities and put us at risk of diluting our efforts.
- *Lowering goals if we fail to achieve them.* Some goals turn out to be overly aggressive—often because we have underestimated the amount of time, level of difficulty, or prevalence of competing priorities.[3] Too often, we lower the bar after hitting the first hurdle, instead of redoubling our efforts to rise to the occasion. Ratcheting goals down should not be the knee-jerk response to initial roadblocks.
- *Not letting our goals see the light of day.* If our goals never make it past the confines of our cranium, they are unlikely to bear fruit in the real world. When Gerald Chertavian decided to launch the non-profit Year Up, he went around to fifty friends at a party in London and evangelized his goals. By going on the record, he made his goals "official" and lent them greater urgency.
- *Letting our goals master us.* Sometimes all the time and energy we pour into accomplishing something evolves into an unhealthy fixation. We need to keep our goals in perspective, maintain flexibility, and celebrate progress along the way. Venture capitalist Randy Komisar advises, "You can't be locked into a rigid sense of objective, because those objectives can become your worst enemies if you're not flexible."

- *Viewing goals as a onetime "sprint."* When goals are quickly set, accomplished, and set aside, they lead to only fleeting success. Properly conceived, goal setting becomes a habit, and goals are pursued through consistent and sustained effort leading to mastery. As George Leonard wrote in his book *Mastery: The Keys to Success and Long-Term Fulfillment,* "Mastery is not about perfection. It's about a process, a journey. The master is the one who stays on the path day after day, year after year. The master is the one who is willing to try, and fail, and try again, for as long as he or she lives."[4]
- *Setting one-dimensional goals.* Many people leap right into goals about a promotion, new job, or diet plan but get tongue-tied when it comes to articulating life goals concerning their family, community, or the like. In addition to his professional goals, Emmet Keeffe also sets personal goals, such as being a great husband and father and remaining physically fit.

Steve Quisenberry, founder of the outdoor equipment company 105 Meridian, owner of Mountainsmith, and former Colorado Entrepreneur of the Year, has always remembered what his mentor told him: "To succeed in life, have a goal." Taking that advice, Steve sets one-, three-, and five-year personal and professional goals each year. His goals have dramatically improved the quality of his life, leading him to move back to Colorado to be close to his parents, reconnect with his church and faith, and sell his business at an opportune time so he could be around and available as a father during his children's formative years. As he says, "I can always go back to work, but I can never re-create this time with my children."

We are wise to beware the common stumbling blocks in setting goals, but they pale in comparison with the biggest danger: not following up goal setting with clear and compelling strategies for accomplishing those goals.

DEVELOPING A STRATEGIC PLAN

Once goals are established, we must devise a plan for how to achieve them. This is the province of strategy. The word *strategy* comes from the Greek *strategos,* a military term that describes the art of the general. In the nineteenth century, military expert Carl von Clausewitz described strategy as "concerned with drafting the plan of war and shaping the individual campaigns."[5] Like a campaign (military, political, or otherwise), an entrepreneurial strategic plan is concerned with achieving a desired vision and set of goals in light of opposing pressures and limited resources. It is a concrete way to organize priorities and direct anticipated actions. In developing a strategic plan, we must do the following:

- Master the context[6]
- Test our assumptions
- Craft experiments
- Remain focused and flexible
- Mitigate risk
- Identify the required resources

MASTERING THE CONTEXT

If we want to change our reality, we must first understand what we are up against. An important first step is comparing our current reality to our goals, being clear about the distance between them and what is required to bridge it.

As it happens, this is where entrepreneurial projects often crash and burn. Mastering the context often means immersing oneself in the applicable environment. It means carefully testing one's concepts and seeking targeted feedback. It requires patience and discipline, penetrating reflection, and brutal honesty. Once we have a clear-eyed view of our current reality and where we want to go, we can begin to identify the gaps in our skills, resources, and relationships, then hatch plans to close those gaps. Many strategic plans include a SWOT analysis: identifying *strengths, weaknesses, opportunities*, and *threats*. This can be helpful at home as well as at work.

There is no magic formula to setting a strategy for a new enterprise or life venture. It is normally a messy, iterative process that moves from breakthrough innovation to important tactics. The "how to" ideas often emerge from a competitive analysis or from benchmarking a related venture. Strategy can also emerge from a *gap analysis* in which we define our current place and where we want to be in five years, and then fill in the steps for how to get there.

If our goal is to open a winery in southern France within two years, for instance, we need to determine the optimal route and the resources required. Of course, we should start with the foundational question of *why* that is our goal—perhaps for lifestyle reasons or to engage in work that we are passionate about. And we should also set a number of subgoals with more refined focus.

Our SWOT analysis may show that our strengths lie in knowing fine wines and running small, family-style restaurants and that there is an opportunity to acquire a fertile piece of land in Provence. However, through an assessment of our weaknesses and potential threats, we concede that we have no experience managing a large-scale vineyard and that there is a real danger of a damaging price war in the industry. That may lead us to a change in strategy: owning a smaller winery that features a country-style restaurant with unique and charming offerings that appeal to local families and upscale travelers.

TESTING OUR ASSUMPTIONS

Once our strategy starts coming into focus, we must validate the underlying assumptions behind our emerging game plan. If the assumptions are not right, the whole enterprise can collapse. Assumption validation requires hardheaded analysis, creative exploration of various scenarios, a study of best practices, and careful financial and operational "due diligence."

For Jared Polis, who had started sixteen companies by the time he was thirty-one, the entrepreneurial process "starts with an idea, but the idea is the easy part. I have many more ideas than I can execute. So then it has to get narrowed to ideas that I'm interested in enough to pursue, and then I study a lot about them."

One of his ideas was Proflowers.com, a direct-to-consumer online flower retailer. Through extensive research on flower growers, existing flower distribution channels, and customer preferences, Jared tested a series of assumptions and concluded that he could avoid the middleman and send flowers directly from the grower to the consumer, preserving freshness while reducing delivery time. The idea took off, and in 2003 the company went public.

CRAFTING EXPERIMENTS

Sometimes the best way to learn about an area of interest is to roll up our sleeves and get directly involved as either a volunteer or an apprenticed "investigator," asking targeted questions along the way: Do my assumptions hold up? Am I ready to dedicate years of my life to this pursuit?

Herminia Ibarra's research on career changes shows that the most successful career changers are people who actively test the waters of new experiences instead of trying to analyze their way to a perfect solution. One of her recommendations for career changers in her book *Working Identity: Unconventional Strategies for Reinventing Your Career* is to "craft experiments": trying out new activities before making any major commitment. As she writes:

> We like to think that the key to a successful career change is knowing what we want to do next, then using that knowledge to guide our actions. But studying people in the throes of the career change process . . . led me to a startling conclusion: Change actually happens the other way around. Doing comes first, knowing second. . . . By far the biggest mistake people make when trying to change careers is delaying the first step until they have settled on a destination. This error is undermining because the only way we figure out what we really want to do is by giving it a try. . . . [This method] tells us to give up the search for a ten-point plan and to accept instead a crooked path. . . . We start by taking action.[7]

When Warren Brown was looking to start a cake business, he took a leave of absence from his legal job to ease into the business through catering. Kimberly Wilson first started teaching yoga classes at night in her living room before opening up her own studio. Murem Sharpe of Evoca advises aspiring entrepreneurs to first work for just a few years with a well-managed company in order to learn key business functions and processes—not a decade, as one used to be advised—and then to work for an entrepreneurial company before launching one in order to prepare for dealing with the often chaotic dynamics of start-ups.

REMAINING FOCUSED AND FLEXIBLE

As we develop our plans, we must make tough choices about where to spend time and resources in pursuit of our goals. Once we decide to go down a certain path, we must also retain flexibility to help us navigate unanticipated events and seize unexpected opportunities. As the saying goes, "No plan survives contact with the enemy." Neither work nor life unfolds in a predictable or linear fashion. Oxford's Richard Pascale, corporate transformation architect and best-selling author, entreats us to "Design, don't engineer. Discover, don't dictate. And decipher, don't presuppose. . . . Living systems cannot be directed along a linear path. Unforeseen consequences are inevitable."[8]

Billy Shore of Share Our Strength admits that his plan for how to run the organization "evolved quite a bit. I've always thought of entrepreneurship as being agile and flexible, listening to what the market tells you, and adapting without compromising your core values." We must be able to recognize mistakes and change strategies when necessary.

This leads us to a paradox: entrepreneurship requires laser focus (including the willingness to make tough choices and stick with it) but also flexibility when "stuff" happens. In this way, it is more art than science. We must navigate this paradox by the compass of our core identity (our purpose and values) and the guiding light of our vision. Although we can be flexible about tactics and approaches, we should identify up front what our nonnegotiables are and hold them close at hand.

MITIGATING RISK

Any entrepreneurial endeavor—whether in business or in life— requires a certain measure of risk. Successful entrepreneurs don't seek risk for its own sake; rather, they use their creativity, resourcefulness, and smarts to mitigate risk by staying alert and crafting backup plans.

Rob Glaser of RealNetworks says, "I'm a risk taker, but to me it's about taking risks where you throw all of your passion in, but you don't ceremonially burn the ships just to say you're in it." For Rob, this meant a significant personal investment to launch RealNetworks—but not enough to bankrupt him and his family.

Larry Leith, founder of the Tokyo Joe's restaurant chain, takes what he calls "smart risks" and aggressively employs risk-mitigation strategies. He explains, "If it's a good idea and I believe in it and there are hurdles to overcome, sometimes I thrive on that. . . . To jump off of a cliff takes courage. But to crawl down the cliff slowly and in a way that is a little more controllable, intelligent, and thought out is probably more 'me.' At the end of the day, if somebody else looks at it and sees you at the bottom, they figure you jumped off the cliff."

For entrepreneurs, there is clearly a spectrum of approaches to risk. The common denominator, though, is effective use of risk-mitigation strategies to help them succeed.

Identifying the Required Resources

A strategic plan is not viable without a corresponding resource strategy. This is as true for a new direction in life as it is for a new enterprise. As we develop a concrete plan for heading in a new direction, we should determine what resources are needed, take an inventory of what resources we have on hand (skills, knowledge, money, time, materials, connections, emotional support, credibility, reputation, access to new relationships, and more), and develop a plan for attracting and mobilizing new resources.[9]

Though each entrepreneurial endeavor has a unique set of resource requirements, there are a few constants to attracting and deploying resources. First, any truly persuasive request for somebody else's time or money requires a strong personal belief, commitment, knowledge, and passion for the cause—as demonstrated by a significant investment of personal "sweat equity." Nothing signals commitment like hard work. Second, as resources are scarce at the beginning of any new initiative, we must allocate our time and limited resources with exceptional discipline. Finally, we must be willing to spend or deploy resources in a timely, proactive way instead of hoarding them.

Too often we use a lack of resources as an excuse for not pursuing our dreams. Life entrepreneurs turn scarce resources to their advantage, putting them in service of achieving their goals, and in turn gaining momentum to attract further resources.

AN INSPIRING ENDEAVOR

Peter Kellner has learned the lessons of effective goal setting and strategic planning firsthand. While in high school in the late 1980s, Peter helped start a student movement proposing a major youth forum on nuclear nonproliferation with national leaders. Their efforts made a big splash, attracting the attention of the national media and prominent politicians.

They also earned the support of Bill Drayton, founder of Ashoka, which has made investments in over 1,800 social entrepreneurs globally. During his meeting with Drayton, Peter recognized the enormous resource and role model that Drayton represented. "It was the first time," he says, "that I realized that the goal to entrepreneurship was essentially empowering others. What does Bill Drayton do? He empowers millions of people. . . . That was the moment that I really developed a philosophy around how one's success really lies in the success of others—others whom you collaborate with and enable. And it all reflects back on you and on them and it's a win-win. That was when I started to come into my own about how to live a life. Still, it isn't easy because there's no real vocational track for that."

Following Drayton's example of focusing internationally, Peter headed off to Eastern Europe after college on a Fulbright scholarship and would regularly call Drayton from Budapest seeking guidance on a number of "crazy, bad ideas." "Here I was over in Hungary," he recalls, "not quite sure what to do with myself. . . . I was insecure about what it was I was trying to achieve. It was extremely undefined."

Peter eventually struck upon some good ideas, including starting a law and policy organization in Hungary (which is still around today) and cofounding an oil services and consultancy company in Russia with a friend (which ultimately sold for $270 million).

While in business school, Peter was introduced (by a friend of Drayton's) to Linda Rottenberg, a dynamic entrepreneur who also happened to be leading Ashoka's expansion into Latin America. He and Linda wrote a business plan to take Ashoka's concept of investing in social entrepreneurs into the private sector. They would call it Endeavor, based on Thoreau's famous quote about elevating our lives through "conscious endeavor."

Meanwhile, Peter had been accepted at Yale Law School. Trying to juggle it all, he deferred his business school studies and spent the next year studying law by day and developing Endeavor's business model by night. He spent that summer in Santiago, Chile, preparing Endeavor for its launch.

En route back to law school in August, Peter scheduled a stopover in Miami to make a pitch to a potential investor (another Drayton connection). Sitting next to him on the plane, by coincidence, was Ashoka's president, Susan Stevenson. After Peter ran his investor pitch for Endeavor by her, she admonished him, "Peter, you have no shot at this happening. You're on leave from business school, you're in the middle of law school, you've only been on the ground for a couple of months, Linda is not about to move to South America, and you're about to go back to school. Who in their right mind is going to get behind you?"

Her articulation of their lack of focus was on point—and struck a deep personal chord. Peter was stunned. "I had a couple hours to think about it," he recalls. "I got off the plane and picked up the phone. It was like six in the morning. I called up my parents and said, 'I'm not going back to Yale.' They said, 'What are you talking about?'"

When Peter made his pitch in Miami, the investor asked him, "So who's going to go do this now?"

Peter replied, "It's interesting you asked, because I've decided to leave graduate school to go build this, and I'm also going to commit more money to it, based on a challenge."

After that, he says, "They stepped out of the room and, I kid you not, five minutes later they walked in and said 'Okay, we're going to support you.' So I got on a plane and flew back to Santiago."

Peter spent the next two years helping Linda build out Endeavor's operations in Chile and Argentina, eventually creating local capacity and a resource network to lead the work going forward. Endeavor has since selected more than 250 entrepreneurs in Latin America, Africa, and Turkey. These entrepreneurs themselves have used their Endeavor selection to leverage their own resources, raising more than $900 million in additional capital and in turn generating $1.9 billion in revenue and almost eighty thousand jobs.[10]

As for Peter, he achieved his goal of finishing up both of his graduate degrees and has continued down an entrepreneurial path. But the lasting impact he wants to have is the one that Bill Drayton played in his life: being an enabler for others' dreams. As he puts it, "What really drives me is the optimism I have about the human condition, that it has so much unrealized potential. . . . How can my efforts enable others to enable others? I believe there's a feedback mechanism occurring when you do that. It's completely reinforcing. . . . For me, it's purposeful enablement of others. . . . I'm most happy when ideas are being generated, people's potential is being illuminated, and things are happening as a consequence."

In his life and work, Peter has been able to accomplish his goals and deploy his strategies largely through critical support from close collaborators like Bill Drayton, Linda Rottenberg, and Susan Stevenson at important junctures. This speaks to the power of cultivating and sustaining a healthy ecosystem of support—the subject of our next chapter.

See www.lifeentrepreneurs.com for exercises related to developing goals and strategies.

PART THREE

BLAZING A TRAIL

CHAPTER SEVEN

BUILDING HEALTHY SUPPORT SYSTEMS

Hiking through the Rocky Mountains in the fall, one can't help but be captivated by the luminescent beauty of aspen leaves. Metamorphosing from dark green to brilliant yellow, they shine brilliantly in the afternoon sun.

Only a few who marvel at the beauty of the leaves, however, know about the remarkable structure that lies underground Born from a single seedling, an entire colony of aspen trees can sprout up through a common root system. Aspens thrive because the root system both nourishes and protects the entire colony. Known as a pioneer species, aspens are often the first tree to sprout after a wildfire. The result is that aspens are both the largest species in the world (with one interconnected aspen root system in the Wasatch Mountains of Utah generating nearly fifty thousand trees over an area of 4.6 million square feet) and the oldest (with one colony estimated to be more than eighty thousand years old).[1] But if the seedling fails to generate a root system, it will not last past the winter.

People are similarly dependent on vibrant networks—more than we realize. We, too, need deep roots, strong support systems, and nourishing resources to grow and flourish through the seasons. In this chapter, we explore the characteristics of healthy support systems; how they are established, cultivated, and maintained; and why they are important.

In our culture, we tend to lionize the heroic individual, often neglecting the essential role that groups and teams have played in our lives and culture. Examples of the latter are legion: the team of Xerox scientists who started the personal computer revolution; the Defense Department teams that launched the Internet; the creative groups in Walt Disney's early studios; the planners (and activists) of the great social movements of our times; the intrepid teams of explorers throughout history; and more.

In *Creating the Good Life,* James O'Toole documents a number of compelling examples of this across time and reflects, "The more I read and thought about it, the 'path-breaking' loner was a myth. . . . In the business world, American corporations are often portrayed as shadows of the 'great men' who sit in chief executive chairs. . . . This individual focus isn't always wrong; rather, it blinds young executives to the existence of other models and causes them to discount the many examples of shared leadership running counter to received wisdom."[2]

There is a growing body of evidence indicating that our support networks and social interactions contribute significantly not only to our success and happiness but also to our health and longevity—from better mental health to lower rates of poor physical health, violence, and mortality.[3] Unfortunately, there is also evidence that our personal support systems are in decline. Robert Putnam famously documented our declining social capital in his landmark work *Bowling Alone.*[4] According to a 2006 study, Americans reported having only two close friends (versus three twenty years ago), one in four reports having nobody with whom to discuss personal issues, and nearly one in ten reports that their spouse is the only person they confide in.[5]

ROOTS AND WINGS

> *There is no such thing as a self-made man. We are made up of thousands of others. Everyone who has ever done a kind deed for us, or spoken one word of encouragement to us, has entered into the make-up of our character and of our thoughts, as well as our success.*
> —GEORGE BURTON ADAMS

As much as we ascribe to the hero's journey, we are more fragile and vulnerable than we care to admit. We need others to fortify our resolve, provide perspective, and buck us up with emotional support. The deepest sources of strength among the life entrepreneurs we interviewed were their life partners, families, friends, mentors, and business partners. These close relationships give us roots and wings—roots to ground us and wings to help us fly.

The important people in our lives encourage us to be a person of character and integrity. They hold our feet to the fire when we drift or waver, help us back on our feet when we stumble, and encourage us to leap when we are ready to soar. They provide us with the all-important emotional foundation that we need to step forward in the world with confidence, willing and able to take risks because our root system is strong.

FAMILY AND FRIENDS

Robert Frost once quipped that "Home is the place where, when you have to go there, they have to take you in." We all share this common point of connection, starting with our immediate and extended families.

Not surprisingly, the influence of parents on the life entrepreneurs we interviewed was unmistakable. In fact, more than 90 percent cited their parents as important influences in their lives, with many learning valuable lessons from them (including lessons about behavior and approaches to avoid). One theme that ran through many of the interviews was parents' influence in instilling the importance of service and contribution. Other strong themes that resonated were the importance of hard work, permission to explore and try new things, support for unconventional approaches and "going their own way," and the importance of chasing dreams. These lessons are now being passed on to future generations of life entrepreneurs.

Our friends also become important influences in our lives, sometimes making up for gaps in our family support system. Our closest friends are our chosen family. True friendships are based on shared values like honesty, understanding, respect, trust, and a reciprocal desire for what is best for the other. Friends listen when no one else will, lend a helping hand, call out our better angels when we are embattled, and push us to new heights.

These friendships can start for the simplest of reasons but are refined like a fine wine over the years—in the process, transforming our lives. An extraordinary life is inconceivable without them. As Abraham Lincoln once proclaimed, "The better part of one's life consists of his friendships."

These days, many of us struggle to find the time for our close relationships. We get lost in days of busyness, with little left to give after hours of the daily grind. After years of leading the NewSchools Venture Fund at a punishing pace, Kim Smith made a dramatic change. "I felt like I had a million transactional relationships and no real relationships," she says, "and that was really not fulfilling for me." Now that she has carved out a new vocation operating at a more sustainable pace, she says, "I'm much more relaxed. I can be a normal person and find a great partner. . . . You need white space in your life so you can have some other things happening in it."

Life Partners and "Entrepreneurial Couples"

Like Kim, many of us realize that we want to connect with one person whom we can count on above all else to guide us, support us, and share life with us with a deep and abiding love. In our interviews, we heard over and over again that life entrepreneurs gain great encouragement, wisdom, perspective, strength, and (sometimes badly needed) humility from their life partners.

This was true for David Carmel of StemCyte: "When you have a strong connection with one thing in your life," he says, "you notice when it is missing in other parts of your life, and you want it more. If you are in a ho-hum job or relationship, it's not obvious what you are missing. But when you are really wowed by your relationship, you begin to realize you want that in your job too." When Howard Schultz was confronted by his father-in-law about his impractical entrepreneurial gambles, his wife, Sheri, stood by him and his vision for what Starbucks could be. When Paul Lightfoot experienced his biggest professional setback during the dot-com bust, his girlfriend (now wife) Karen told him, "You didn't fail, your business did. I don't have any problem with this."

In writing this book, we were struck by the number of "entre-preneurial couples" we came across, in which both partners are engaged in entrepreneurial pursuits in work, life, or both. We suspect that there may be a trend here of people creating extraordinary lives together based on shared values and common passions.

Linda Mason and Roger Brown have been married for twenty years. Together, they cofounded the child-care provider Bright Horizons and created and ran significant humanitarian relief organizations in Asia and Africa, forging a partnership that spans all areas of their lives. Linda says, "For us it has been great. We are extremely compatible. We have an enormous amount of respect for each other, and it adds this extra dimension to our relationship. It's just incredibly rich to create an organization together. . . . Through all the very difficult start-up years, we had each other to lean on and celebrate our successes together. . . . It has really just worked."

When Paul Nasrani was launching his new ice-cream business, he started dating Simi Mir. He recounts, "She came up that first summer and helped me. It was really hard. We were cleaning machines until four in the morning. That September, I went to India with her to work on her documentary [on the relationship between Kashmiri Muslims and Hindus]. I thought, *This is so great. We're helping each other with our dreams.* I loved it when Simi started her own law firm. It was nuts to go to zero income, but all of a sudden she and I had the same problems. We really understood what it's like for each other. I think one of the reasons we are together—one of many reasons—is that this is an exciting thing about each of us. She says 'I want to do something' and she just goes and does it. Anything's possible."

David Gray and Bridget Bradley Gray credit each other for helping them make big changes in their lives. Bridget supported David when he entered the ministry, and David reciprocated when Bridget left a non-profit position to start her own business. For David, it provides a "feeling of confidence to take risks." He calls this "the dance of being rooted while spreading my wings" and says that "the bedrock that makes everything else possible is my wife." Bridget adds, "Being true to our relationship has opened up opportunities, allowing us to dream. . . . Goals are no longer in terms of our title or salary but in terms of what makes us happy. . . . It's empowering. It would be difficult if one of us wasn't in that place. It's powerful because we're both feeling excited about where we are, even outside our relationship. That's probably not a coincidence."

The growth of such "entrepreneurial couples" may be a budding cultural phenomenon. We believe it warrants further study as our society increasingly turns to entrepreneurship as a catalyst of personal wealth, social progress, and happiness.

> *A life without love, without the presence of the*
> *beloved, is nothing but a mere magic-lantern show.*
> *We draw out each slide after slide, swiftly tiring of*
> *each, and pushing it back to make haste for the next.*
> —GOETHE

MENTORS

Along the entrepreneurial path, mentors can have a profound effect on our outlook on and approach to life. The term *mentor* comes from Greek mythology, and its prevalence in our lives appears universal—from Aristotle's mentorship of Alexander the Great to bicyclist Eddy Merckx's mentorship of Lance Armstrong. Author Eric Liu calls these trusted friends, counselors, and teachers our "guiding lights."[6]

Many of the life entrepreneurs we interviewed relied on mentors at critical junctures in their lives. According to Carl Schramm, president of the Kauffman Foundation, "Studies show that the rate of success of a new business start-up can be improved by a factor of at least three if the entrepreneur has a mentor. . . . All entrepreneurs can benefit from mentors. . . . The best mentors are people who failed once or twice and had many difficulties in the birthing of their companies."[7] Being a mentor is something for life entrepreneurs themselves to aspire to, given the opportunity for impact and contribution that it provides.

Technology entrepreneur Randy Komisar's mentor, Bill Campbell, has had a profound and lasting effect on his life. Formerly head football coach at Columbia University, "Coach" Campbell led Apple's effort to spin off its software applications group, calling it Claris Corporation. Because of Bill's reputation for integrity and talent development, Randy tracked him down. Within minutes of their first meeting, Randy was recruited onto the new company's executive team—a move that put him on the fast track in Silicon Valley. In the process, Randy gained a lifelong coach and friend.[8] He reflects, "Mentorship to me is a very special relationship, and those are rare. Mentors are not on every street corner. A mentor is somebody who can provide you with the benefit of their wisdom and experience in the context of allowing you to be who you are, and who you are becoming." Following a common pattern of protégés becoming mentors themselves, Randy has since provided karmic reciprocity by mentoring a host of start-up founders.

Sometimes collegial mentoring is fostered by organized groups. Today, organizations like Net Impact, Social Venture Network, Young Presidents Organization, Business Roundtable, Chamber of Commerce, and others serve this purpose. For example, Kim Smith benefited greatly from the Aspen Institute's Crown Fellows program, in which twenty emerging leaders from across the country convene in Aspen, Colorado, for seminars focused on values-based leadership to enhance their intellectual and personal development, culminating in community leadership projects. "Part of the Crown experience," she explains, "is having real time to reflect. The people there were really exceptional people coming from different angles, and there was a lot of commonality around the types of things we were wrestling with as leaders. When you're leading an organization, you find that you end up without very many people to talk to about what you need. It was nice to process my own personal thinking around leadership with a group of people who had no stake in it other than being my thought partners, as colleagues and fellows."

Other life entrepreneurs have created their own mentoring or support groups. Paul Lightfoot, founder of Food Line and CEO of AL Systems, has created his "personal board of directors," which he convenes occasionally to discuss his life goals and the world at large. As he explains, "I believe that the people that you surround yourself with are the most important factor in the quality of life. There are people I seek out just to feel better about the world. I also like the idea of being held accountable. I can tell people what my goals are, and then I feel like I'm accountable to someone besides myself."

PROFESSIONAL PARTNERSHIPS

Many enterprises thrive under the leadership of a team, especially in partnerships where a shared sense of accountability is matched with a common passion. Many of the most successful life entrepreneurs we interviewed had found other life entrepreneurs with whom to pool their efforts toward a shared vision. In our experience, the best partnerships arise from integrity; trust; open communication; mutual commitment to a common purpose, values, and vision; and complementary skills and personalities.

As a consultant on the fast track at Mercer Consulting, Rajiv Vinnakota started thinking about the "social footprint he was going to leave." Motivated by his volunteer work in the schools of Washington, D.C., and a strong service ethic in his family, he engaged his friends in conversations about how he could make a difference.

In the process, Raj became intrigued with the novel idea of creating publicly funded boarding schools for urban youth. Inspired by the possibilities, he took a leave of absence to explore its feasibility. Not one to do things in half measures, he traveled around the country visiting private boarding schools and meeting with educators, policymakers, and urban community leaders. While gathering information, he was also building an impressive network of contacts in the field.

One day, he got a call out of the blue from Eric Adler, who was at a rival consulting firm but ready to embark on his own entrepreneurial life journey. Previously, Eric had taught for eight years at an independent day school. While teaching, he wondered, *What if I could do my own thing? What if I could create this kind of experience for kids who can't afford the benefits of a private school?* As he began resurrecting that aspiration, he was connected to Raj through a mutual friend.

When they got together, Raj and Eric spent hours brainstorming over burgers. A few weeks later, Raj convened a group at a weekend retreat to discuss the possibilities. After an intensive weekend, everybody but Raj and Eric went back to their respective lives.

They stayed behind and surveyed all they had drawn up, realizing that it would take at least two people full-time to make it work. That day, a partnership was born.

The next day, though they had met only twice, they walked into their respective firms and resigned. Together, they created the SEED Foundation in Washington, D.C., which runs an impressive inner-city boarding school and was awarded the prestigious Innovations in Government Award in 2005. The school serves more than three hundred students in grades seven to twelve on a four-building campus and includes not only college-prep academic programs but also life skills programs, college and career counseling, and athletics and extracurricular programs. Raj and Eric are now seeking to replicate this model in other cities across the country.

The school continues to benefit from their entrepreneurial approach to building and leveraging a support network. They have been systematic about developing partnerships with a mind-boggling array of local and national community organizations as well as sophisticated fund-raising campaigns, including a successful effort to secure a sizable federal appropriation from the U.S. Congress for the school.

Their partnership has also produced a deep friendship. As Raj says, "Our partnership and friendship have been very important. . . . It made me more entrepreneurial in having someone else to bounce ideas off of—someone who challenges me, and who thinks about issues differently. . . . I don't think SEED would be here if I was the only one doing it."

> When we are in this state of being where we are open to life and all its possibilities, willing to take the next step as it is presented to us, then we meet the most remarkable people who are important contributors to our life.
> —Joseph Jaworski, *Synchronicity*

Extended Networks of Support

Beyond establishing close circles of support, life entrepreneurs also cultivate relationships outside their immediate comfort zone. We are wise to foster relationships with a wide array of people who can guide our journey—providing us with alternative perspectives, diverse counsel, specific knowledge, targeted introductions to others who can help us, and thoughtful guidance.

Building our support network must not become an exercise in selfishness or narcissism. Rather, it is about building support for a shared vision and asking people to join us on the journey, even as we help others as best we can. The point is to pull together trusted relationships in pursuit of something lasting and worthy. Psychologist David Berlew asserts that humans are bonded by a common set of "value-related opportunities": a chance to be tested, a chance to do something well, a chance to do something good, and a chance to change the ways things are.[9] Our entrepreneurial journey is an opportunity to invite people to join this endeavor and accomplish remarkable things together.

HOW TO BUILD A STRONG SUPPORT NETWORK

As we seek help from the array of people and groups just mentioned, we need to be able to communicate why help is needed, how people can help, and why they might be interested in doing so. Being able to articulate a clear and inspiring vision is an essential component of life entrepreneurship. To encourage people to join in our mission, we must be able to ignite their interest and earn their support.

Persuasion begins with authenticity. When we aren't speaking from personal conviction and conveying passion, our words ring hollow. Part of this persuasion also comes from giving people confidence that we have done our homework—with a clear sense of what we know and what we don't know. This speaks to humility. "To know the road ahead," says the Chinese proverb, "ask those coming back." Asking for support should be followed by deep listening and learning as well as respect for the person's time and experience. Sometimes, this requires accepting tough feedback and a willingness to go back to the drawing board. Most important, we must acknowledge the assistance that was provided, give credit where credit is due, and engage in strong, personal follow-up.

Will Pearson figured this out remarkably early. When he was a sophomore at Duke University, he and his buddies would cram into a dorm room for late-night conversations. Often, they talked about their classes—and how hard it was to get a basic handle on any of the disciplines, despite all their hard work. They wondered what they were really learning and how useful it would be in the real world. They also marveled at how it was that they could be so engaged when they used modern communications gizmos but so bored to tears with their academic texts.

Will sensed an opportunity and started brainstorming with his friend, Mangesh Hattikudur, about how to address these problems in innovative ways. Together, they envisioned an on-campus magazine that would be both educational and entertaining for their fellow students and potentially for a much larger audience. The big idea was to create ways for people to learn interesting and relevant things in a fun way, allowing them both to feel smarter and enjoy the process.

After conducting exhaustive research on the magazine industry, they pitched the university's Undergraduate Publication Board and the various academic departments on their idea to try to secure start-up funds. Impressed with the amount of research Will and Mangesh had conducted, Duke supported their efforts. Not long afterward, the inaugural issue of *mental_floss* hit the campus bookstores.

Recognizing the need for expert guidance, they found a Mississippi professor who was knowledgeable about magazine publishing and willing to lead them through the steps of a magazine's start-up, from design and printing to legal and distribution. Will recalls, "It was incredible to have an advisor. . . . One of the smartest things we did early was rather than focus on all of the articles and design, the first step was research, and the second step was setting up conversations with as many experts in the industry as we possibly could." They leveraged their own contacts, including family and friends, plus the resources of the Duke alumni network and spent hundreds of hours reaching out and asking for their help.

In the end, these ambitious college students put together an advisory board for their fledgling magazine that included former editors from *Time* and *Newsweek*. Will recalls, "It took hundreds of phone calls and e-mails and letters and whatever we needed to do, and then in those conversations to truly convey not only a passion for this but the fact that we had really done our homework and that we were serious."

Will scrapped his plans for studying abroad to focus on the magazine. After publishing a couple of issues on campus, they were ready to make the leap to national newsstands. Through their budding network, they made contacts with independent distributors, negotiated test markets, and landed meetings with Borders and Barnes & Noble. Then their big break arrived: a *Washington Post* review of their magazine (they had courted the newspaper for this) was picked up nationwide in other publications. Seizing the momentum, they again tapped their network to get meetings with investors and secured funding for a year.

The magazine business is famously fickle, though, and they wondered whether they could make a viable long-term business out of *mental_floss.* Their subscriber base was already showing signs of leveling off. The more they talked to advisors and industry leaders, the more ideas came their way for how they could transform their magazine into a broader media platform. One advisor suggested that they could turn their concept into a book, and she made an introduction that led to a book deal. Due to all the buzz they had generated, CNN approached them about doing a weekly program.

As of this writing, the magazine *mental_floss* has about three hundred thousand regular readers, and they have seven books in print, a contract for a children's book series, a board game, a series of calendars, a T-shirt line, and a robust website and blog— not to mention partnerships with AOL, CNN, Discovery, *Readers Digest,* and others.

How did these twenty-somethings turn those late-night dormroom bull sessions into gold? Will reflects, "One of our advisory board members told us, 'I think the reason this has worked is because you were too young to realize what you couldn't do.'" It was a classic example of a "beginner's mind" wrapped up with a healthy "disregard for the impossible." But what proved invaluable was their strategic approach to building a support network. By reaching out with such discipline and tenacity, they were able to generate opportunity, fresh ideas, buzz, credibility, partnerships, and funding, plus a large number of new friends, colleagues, and mentors along the way.

As Will and Mangesh learned, our support networks are built one relationship at a time. The question is, *how* do we build support networks of quality and integrity? There are ample tools today to help us with the *quantity* of people in our network. With the advent of peer-to-peer social networking sites like Flickr, MySpace, Facebook, and SixDegrees, we can connect to vast networks of people from Beirut to Bali. As we write, LinkedIn, one of the leading sites, boasts eight million member profiles—mostly from outside the United States. In 2005, an average person with just twenty contacts could connect with an estimated forty thousand members within four degrees of separation.[10]

There is a caveat, though. The strength of our support network is only as good as the quality of its relationships. In his best-selling book *The Seven Habits of Highly Effective People,* Stephen R. Covey emphasizes the importance of our "emotional bank account." As with a traditional bank account, we can build up our account over time with deposits, in this case through "courtesy, kindness, honesty, and keeping commitments."[11]

"Authentic" Networking

As we build our support network, we must each develop an approach that is genuine, authentic, and aligned with our nature and values. When Larry Leith, founder of the hip and successful Tokyo Joe's "fast fresh" restaurant chain in Denver, worked in the ski industry—first as a professional skier and then for a ski gear company—he met a parade of heavy-hitting CEOs. He was invited to fancy dinners and exotic locales around the world. But he wasn't pursuing any of it as networking. He explains, "All those friendships were honest, and I have all of those friendships still. . . . I think if it had been the other way around, it would have been different. That word, 'network': I don't think it works that way. I think it is spontaneous. There has to be a connection there. If you're trying to do things for these people, to suck up, they pick it out. I'm in that position now, and I can read right through it." That was a lesson he learned from mentors.

Larry has built a successful enterprise with integrity and flair. But it almost never happened. When he began, the "fast casual" craze hadn't hit yet, and he had a hard time getting a lease for his first restaurant. He recalls that he went two years with no income as he chased his dream: "I got told 'no' so many times. I was desperate and out of money. I charged my house payment on my credit card. I stalked the landlord to get the deal done. I literally cornered him in his office, and, I think out of embarrassment, he signed the lease that night."

Meanwhile, Larry had been cooking every night and honing his craft. His big break arrived when a friend and mentor stepped in with a big investment and told him, "If you lose this money, we'll still be friends." Even now, Larry says, "We don't have any legal documents between us. Everything is done out of mutual respect."

When Tokyo Joe's opened, they had a line out the door on the third day, and he hasn't looked back since. Today, they serve about fifty thousand customers a week in the Denver metro area. Much of their success comes from how they treat their people. According to Larry:

> Through the years, Joe's has been known as a really great place
> to work. I laugh when somebody says they're an equal opportu-
> nity employer. Well, *duh*. We're beyond that. We're an *open-minded*
> employer. Our motto is "The few, the proud, the pierced." We have
> benefited from having fabulous people who, for a variety of reasons
> in their own lifestyles, may have limited some of the places willing
> to take a risk on them. . . . We promote people to manager early.
> We take those risks with people. And most often it works out really
> well. They grow in their own personal life exponentially, just like
> I have. Treating them as an equal, being straight with them, and
> giving them these opportunities and encouragements has been
> huge for us.

TRUST, DIVERSITY, AND RECIPROCITY

There are several common themes in the approaches that life entrepreneurs take in building healthy support systems: trust, diversity, and reciprocity. Let's take a brief look at each of these.

THE POWER OF TRUST

Trust is fundamental in any relationship. If people trust us, they are more likely to introduce us to others, share new ideas, and invest in our development. Trust comes from integrity. According to Randy Komisar, "If you strive towards excellence, do great work, and live with integrity, you will earn the relationships that you will need to be successful." Information flows quickly and easily between people who trust one another. Stephen M. R. Covey calls this "the speed of trust."[12]

Mark Warner has learned about the power of trust during his distinguished career. The first member of his family to graduate from college, he headed off to Harvard Law School and then went to work for the Democratic National Committee "for $18,000 a year," he recalls, "probably a quarter of what my classmates were getting when they graduated in 1980."

That work exposed him to a number of entrepreneurs. Inspired by their example, he took his savings of $5,000 and invested it in a start-up energy company, despite the fact that his college loans were coming due. Within six weeks, the company went belly-up. From there, he pursued another venture that bombed, this time after six months. He recalls, "I went out to be an entrepreneur and failed miserably twice. At the ripe old age of twenty-six, I was flat broke, living out of my car, and sleeping on friends' couches."

Undeterred, he learned through relationships on Capitol Hill about a promising opportunity to bid on cellular licenses. Through contacts in Connecticut, he landed a meeting to pitch a self-made millionaire named David Chase on investing in the licenses. Thirty minutes into Warner's pitch, Chase agreed to invest a million dollars. Warner then tapped his law school network to get a meeting with the Washington Post Company, which also agreed to join the deal. That deal set the stage for a number of cell phone ventures, eventually leading to the creation of Nextel—and Warner's financial (and political) fortunes. He went on to build a track record as a successful entrepreneur and to become governor of Virginia. As he reflects, "Early on, there was nothing I did that wasn't the result of somebody believing in me enough to take a risk on me." He had built up a bank account of trust.

Following his big splashes in the cell phone industry, Warner cofounded a venture capital firm that was financed entirely by the investments from the five partners. No legal documents were drawn up between them. "We all operated on basic trust and respect for each other," recalls Warner. They also carried this approach into their outside business deals: "We had the philosophy that there was always going to be another deal, so making the last nickel off of every deal wasn't the most important thing. . . . [The fact] that people believed that we were going to shoot straight with them and be fair with them was the most valuable asset in the long run. I think a really good entrepreneur is somebody who realizes that you've got to create a win-win."

DIVERSITY: CROSSING BOUNDARIES

We also need to inject diversity into our support systems by crossing boundaries, establishing relationships outside of our comfort zone. By connecting to people and networks that are diverse—in terms of outlook, geography, industry, income, status, age, gender, race, ethnicity, religion, and more—our world gets thrown open to a whole new set of possibilities and creative inputs, bringing us fresh perspective. As organizational design experts Brian Uzzi and Shannon Dunlap write, "Highly diverse network ties can help you develop more complete, creative, and unbiased views of issues."[13]

According to John Sculley, former president of PepsiCo and CEO of Apple, "One of the biggest mistakes a person can make is to put together a team that reflects only him. I find it's better to put teams together of people who have different skills and then make all those disparate skills function together. The real role of the leader is to figure out how you make diverse people and elements work together."

For starters, we must examine the diversity of our support network. Are we limiting our perspective by consulting with the same people from similar backgrounds again and again? If so, we must look for ways to change it up. Also, it can often be enormously helpful if we connect the dots between our networks, acting as a conduit between groups. Networks are traditionally self-contained and isolated. When they are connected, a whole new set of relationships opens up. Additionally, many new opportunities are usually made available to the original "connector," perpetuating and accelerating the cycle.

When Kim Smith entered the education sector, there was a gaping chasm between the world of venture capital and the education sector. Because she had experience and relationships across both realms, she was able to bridge those disparate worlds. While at Stanford Business School, Kim met John Doerr and Brook Byers of the venerable Kleiner Perkins Caufield & Byers venture capital group. Having made early investments in America Online (AOL), Netscape, and Amazon (earning a 55,000 percent return), they were interested in how properly capitalized social entrepreneurs could make a difference in the nation's public schools.

When they met Kim, two worlds converged. The result was a new kind of investment vehicle for the education community. To date, NewSchools Venture Fund (NSVF) has invested over $60 million in promising education enterprises using an innovative "venture philanthropy" strategy. As the primary broker in this relationship, Kim was asked to run NSVF, which flourished under her leadership. Much of her success can be attributed to her ability to earn the trust of key associates and build bridges across diverse networks.

RECIPROCITY AND THE "POSITIVE NETWORK EFFECT"

The final element of building long-standing relationships and quality support systems is reciprocity. As Emmet B. Keeffe III, cofounder and CEO of iRise, expressed during our interview, "I think human beings fundamentally want to help other people, and I am constantly reaching out to people for help. . . . And if they help me, they know that they can always call me for help." Being willing to give back is an essential part of any lasting relationship.

Mary Cutrufello was a rising music star in the nineties when a band called Reckless Kelly came to Texas from Idaho. Recalling what it was like when she tried to break into the music scene in the Lone Star State, she introduced them to the local scene and wrote the liner notes for their first album. For the newcomers, it was a big break.

Years later, when Mary was trying to make a comeback after being sidelined, Reckless Kelly offered to sing on her comeback album, invited her to jam with them at a high-profile music festival, and interviewed her for their documentary. "They did me a major solid," Mary recalls. "I've been away for a long time. It's a long game, as we used to say. Stuff does come back around, people do remember. I always believed that if you do the right thing, then it kind of has its own momentum."

This theme echoed throughout many of our interviews. When we are doing something good in the world that people want to support, they not only lend a hand but also recruit others to do the same. A splash ripples outward, and the power of the shared vision becomes stronger with every concentric circle. We call this the *positive network effect:* when a positive idea flows through a broad web of relationships, the power of the idea gains momentum, sometimes becoming unstoppable. It is the key ingredient to taking an idea from vision to reality. It is the fuel that has driven social and political movements throughout history. When we work together in good faith on worthy endeavors, our root systems become interconnected, creating a unified effort further strengthened to make a lasting difference in the world.

> *Few will have the greatness to bend history; but each of us can work to change a small portion of events, and in the total of all those acts will be written the history of this generation. It is from numberless diverse acts of courage and belief that human history is thus shaped. Each time a man stands up for an ideal, or acts to improve the lot of others, or strikes out against injustice, he sends forth a tiny ripple of hope, and crossing each other from a million different centers of energy and daring, those ripples build a current which can sweep down the mightiest walls of oppression and resistance.*
> —ROBERT KENNEDY

CHAPTER EIGHT

TAKING ACTION AND MAKING A DIFFERENCE

You miss 100 percent of all the shots you never take.
—WAYNE GRETZKY

Entrepreneur = the *acting person*. Ultimately, the defining moment for a life entrepreneur is when she puts away her lingering doubts, rolls up her sleeves, and goes for it.

As Erma Bombeck said, "There are people who put their dreams in a little box and say, 'Yes, I've got dreams, of course. I've got dreams.' Then they put the box away and bring it out once in a while to look in it, and yep, they're still there. These are great dreams, but they never even get out of the box. It takes an uncommon amount of guts to put your dreams on the line, to hold them up and say, 'How good or bad am I?' That's where the courage comes in."

THE COURAGE TO TRY

*Courage is not the absence of fear, but the capacity
for action despite our fears.*
—JOHN MCCAIN

Often, what is most essential in creating an extraordinary life is what is needed to get started. We call this the *courage to try:* courage to discover who we really are and leave what is comfortable, safe, and known. Courage to act on our convictions.

Courage to see our dreams played out against the backdrop of the world. Courage to fail. Courage simply to begin.

For Anita Sharpe, courage meant walking away from a prestigious job at the *Wall Street Journal* at the pinnacle of her career to pursue her calling and start a magazine and company focused on helping people pursue worthwhile work and lives. For Cory Booker, it was leaving behind a world of comfort and moving to a housing project in Newark to join the front lines of a battle against poverty. For Mary Cutrufello, it was about reviving her musical career after being sidelined for years by illness. For Karin Weber, it was reinventing her life at sixty and embracing all sorts of new adventures. These life entrepreneurs acted in spite of their fears. Indeed, without fear, courage is impossible.

We often confine our thinking about courage to fields of battle and acts of valor. But there is also a personal courage that requires a willingness to start taking action even in small ways that get us moving in the right direction.

WINDOWS OF OPPORTUNITY

In any entrepreneurial venture, timing is everything. A window of opportunity can close as quickly as it opens. In business, these windows open and close with changing customer preferences, new technologies, competitor moves, fluctuations in the market, and more. In our personal lives, windows of opportunity open more often than we think—when we meet someone who shares our values or passions, get a chance to make a difference in someone's life, or get invited to climb a mountain—but they can close just as quickly. The key is to recognize these opportunities when they appear and be ready to seize them.

Windows of opportunity are fickle. When they open up, we don't always recognize it at first, and we almost never know when they are going to close. Jump too soon and risk landing short of the destination. Spend too much time in preparation mode ("analysis paralysis") and the opportunity may have passed. Once an opportunity is spotted, an idea vetted, we must decide: take action or walk away. Wallowing in indecision results in missed opportunities and the potential for regret (see Figure 8.1).

FIGURE 8.1. THE WINDOW OF OPPORTUNITY.

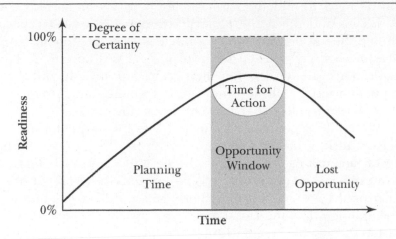

Sometimes opportunity presents itself before we feel ready. Questions then arise: Is this a once-in-a-lifetime opportunity that we will regret passing up? Can we keep our options open while we scramble to become more knowledgeable and better prepared? We rarely have all the information we would like. The best we can do is to be as prepared as possible. "The secret of success in life," Benjamin Disraeli once said, "is for a man to be ready for his time when it comes."

PURPOSEFUL SPONTANEITY

As a child, Paul Nasrani worked at a rustic family farm where they used to make homemade ice cream to celebrate a good harvest or a hard day's work—pretty much whatever excuse they could find. He spent his summers on Lake George's Silver Bay, a beloved family retreat community and conference center in the Adirondack Mountains of upstate New York. For Paul, those memories were soaked with bliss. When he was twelve, he was troubled to learn that the Silver Bay resort had fallen upon hard times, so he resolved to open up an ice-cream company and give the ice cream away for free to help.

As he grew older, he filed the notion of opening an ice-cream company away in his childhood dream box and only occasionally let it peek out. After college, he took a job with an audit and consulting firm and then worked for a series of start-up companies up and down the eastern seaboard in a CFO capacity. Though he was helping others launch their entrepreneurial ventures, he hadn't yet taken his own plunge. "I'd have these great inspirations," he recalls, "but then go back to my job, and they'd just get buried. I really lost the vision of what I wanted to do for a while. When you lose that, it's very discomforting."

When the September 11 attacks hit in his adopted home city of New York, it moved him to open up his dream box and act. He began making ice cream at home and voraciously learning about the ice-cream industry: visiting dozens of ice-cream stores, quizzing the owners, touring dairy farms and factories, and even researching what industrial ice-cream machines cost. And he started sharing his dream with others.

On a quiet Sunday in January 2004, he was working alone in his office in New York City and ducked out to grab a bite to eat. At Grand Central Station, Paul was surprised to see that his favorite ice-cream store was going out of business—and that it was auctioning off its assets right then and there, including an industrial ice-cream maker like the ones he had been researching.

Should I put in a bid?

The thought was tantalizing—but ridiculously impractical. The machine must have weighed eight hundred pounds, and he couldn't be sure that it still worked. And something about the auction seemed shady. But this unlikely convergence of events felt to him like "the hand of God," he later said.

Before he knew it, he was pushing this hulking machine down 42nd Street, wondering where in the world he was going to store it. On that day, Adirondack Creamery was born. (A few days later, he went on a date with Simi, a friend of a friend who had caught his eye, and confessed what he had done. That act of boldness—or tomfoolery—captured her attention. Two years later, they were married at Silver Bay.)

Paul's actions exemplify what we call *purposeful spontaneity:* taking action that is unplanned—even impulsive—but also deeply in synch with our core identity. Mythologist Joseph Campbell says that when you "follow your bliss . . . you put yourself on a kind of track that has been there all the while, waiting for you. . . . When you can see that, you begin to meet people who are in the field of your bliss, and they open the doors for you. I say, follow your bliss and don't be afraid, and doors will open where you didn't know they were going to be."[1]

Like Paul, life entrepreneurs are prepared when windows of opportunity are thrown open. What makes it possible is recognizing when those opportunities are aligned with the deep sense of purpose we feel in our bones—followed by the willingness to pounce on those opportunities in an instant of courage, inspiration, and improvisation.

IN THE ARENA

> *It is not the critic who counts; not the man who*
> *points out how the strong man stumbled, or*
> *where the doer of deeds could have done them better.*
> *The credit belongs to the man who is actually in the*
> *arena, who strives valiantly . . . who knows the great*
> *enthusiasms, the great devotions . . . and spends*
> *himself in a worthy . . . cause, who at the best,*
> *knows the triumph of high achievement; and who,*
> *at the worst, if he fails . . . at least fails while daring*
> *greatly, so that his place shall never be with those*
> *cold and timid souls . . . who know neither victory*
> *nor defeat.*
> —THEODORE ROOSEVELT

At some point, all life entrepreneurs have to enter the arena—all the better while "daring greatly." According to start-up mentor Randy Komisar, "In that moment where you've decided this is what you're going to do, you do it with everything you've got. There is no hedging involved. You apply yourself fully and you do your best." Goethe tells us that "the moment that one definitely commits one's self, then Providence moves, too."

When we are launching a new enterprise or taking a new direction in life, chaos often reigns supreme. We rapidly transition from a stroll to a sprint. Pushing forward from the starting blocks is often the most vulnerable stage. At that point, we have limited resources, an unproven concept, no track record, and stress brought on by uncertainty.

As such, life entrepreneurs are wise to prioritize "early wins." Wins beget wins and limit the fallout from our inevitable missteps. For Mary Cutrufello's comeback in the cutthroat music scene, early wins entailed releasing a new album and rebuilding her confidence. As she says, "Making the record was huge. It was even more fulfilling than I anticipated it would be. . . . A lot of it is as simple as making a conscious effort to put yourself there."

Staying there, once we have made the leap, requires both hard work and a focus on excellence. It is about doing whatever it takes—within our core values—for however long it takes to make our effort successful. It is about discipline, focus, and elbow grease. And when our dreams are realized through hard work, they are the sweeter for it.

But no amount of elbow grease can help us carry the day without an ample dose of quality in our actions. This brings us to excellence—the state of being good at something to a high degree. As we change careers, pursue audacious goals, or set off in new directions, we should strive for a higher standard of performance in matters that we deem important, not settling for "good enough." The key is to build this pride of action into our modus operandi, adopting the habit of acting at our very best as often as possible and especially when it really counts. By doing so, we can attain the deeper satisfaction that comes from fulfilling our potential. "We are what we repeatedly do," says Aristotle. "Excellence, then, is not an act, but a habit."

According to Tom Peters, coauthor of *In Search of Excellence*, "We got it right when we said we were in search of excellence. . . . [It's] about heart. About beauty. It's about art. About people throwing themselves on the line. It's about passion and the selfless pursuit of an ideal."[2]

PERVASIVE SERVICE

This is the true joy in life—the being used for a purpose recognized by yourself as a mighty one, the being a force of nature instead of a feverish, selfish little clod of ailments and grievances, complaining that the world will not devote itself to making you happy. I am of the opinion that my life belongs to

the whole community and as long as I live, it is my
privilege to do for it whatever I can.
—GEORGE BERNARD SHAW

At our best, as life entrepreneurs we integrate the broader concept of service into everything we do through our relationships and actions. This approach is grounded in recognition that our lives have impact. Service is not something that is compartmentalized or relegated to an occasional good deed. Rather, it shows up in nearly every aspect of our lives. Service becomes an organizing principle of the entrepreneurial life, an aspiration that pervades our family lives, work lives, and whatever else we do. As Marian Wright Edelman shares with us, "Service is the very purpose of life. It is the rent we pay for living on the planet."

Of course, we live in a world of practicality, with families to support and bills to pay, but the rewards of service are many, and prioritizing it may not be as difficult as we think. When we approach it creatively and expansively, we devise countless opportunities to serve in enlightened ways. According to Benjamin Franklin, "The noblest question in the world is, *What good may I do in it?*" When we invoke that mind-set, we stumble onto new ideas and exciting opportunities to make a contribution in the ways we live and the ways we act.

Buie Seawell, now a wildly popular professor at the University of Denver, has had a wide-ranging career worthy of a Renaissance man: attorney, theologian, pastor, professor, and political leader. He ran his own political research company, led the Colorado Office of Energy Conservation, was a candidate for U.S. Senate, headed up the Colorado Democratic Party, and served on the senior staff of a Colorado governor and a U.S. senator.

Throughout his life, he has sought to be "at the cutting edge of what's happening in the world," he says. "I just had this drive, this imperative, to be connected with what was happening in the way the world was changing." In fact, he has been a part of the civil rights movement (including marching with Dr. Martin Luther King Jr.), the environmental movement, and today's burgeoning movement for business ethics and corporate social responsibility.

Born the son of a preacher, Buie learned the importance of service from his family in small-town North Carolina: "Dad was very clear about that," he recalls. "He had a very simple notion. He didn't understand people who attempted private lives or lives of just doing their job and only being with their family. Private life is important, but it cannot be exclusive, because the only way that government of, for, and by the people works is by people being a part of it."

Reflecting on his own life of service, he explains in his quiet deep drawl, "I think of it as a resonance. Certain realities, certain places, certain movements resonated with who I felt myself to be. I could feel them when I got close to them. I mean, I would have followed Martin King to hell. If Bobby Kennedy had not been shot, I would have been proud to be the trash emptier at the White House. . . . And in the desiring of justice, in the desiring of fairness, in the desire of serving, I had been lucky to be with people who had an extraordinary vision as to how that could be fulfilled."

Today, he's back to doing what he loves—teaching—and preparing his young charges for when their time comes. "I have a passion for what I do that I can't live without," he explains. "I do think there are occasions and opportunities for service that will vary throughout anyone's life. The initial gate is that you understand that that's a piece of being a full person. It's a matter of saying yes to the opportunity when it appropriately appears. Every day is a preparation for serving something."

Like Buie, we should strive to realize a powerful consistency of action on behalf of things larger than our selves. One of Buie's heroes provides an inspiring example:

> Every now and then I think about my own death, and I think about my own funeral. And if you get somebody to deliver the eulogy, tell them not to talk too long. Tell them not to mention that I have a Nobel Peace Prize. Tell them not to mention that I have three or four hundred other awards. I'd like for somebody to say some day that Martin Luther King Jr. tried to give his life serving others.
> —MARTIN LUTHER KING JR.

In *The Cathedral Within*, Billy Shore of Share Our Strength invokes the metaphor of cathedral building to illuminate the essence of service, demonstrating that we can transform our lives by giving something back.[3] He marvels that some of the world's greatest cathedrals took hundreds of years to build, with some people dedicating their entire lives to a project that was so large they knew they could never finish it in their lifetimes. Yet they persisted, inspired by a dream that would outlive them. Shore challenges us all to find a lasting and worthy cause to dedicate our lives to, as he has with his entrepreneurial humanitarian work, and in the process to construct our own cathedral within.

ADAPTIVE PERSISTENCE

One man scorned and covered with scars still strove with his last ounce of courage to reach the unreachable stars; and the world was better for this.
—MIGUEL DE CERVANTES, *DON QUIXOTE*

When life entrepreneurs get going, they often break with convention and meet resistance. What marks the successful life entrepreneur is relentless persistence, a refusal to give up when things go south. But that doesn't mean being bullheaded and knocking on the same door over and over. It means going around the back door one day and the side door the next until we find the right way in.

Persistence is about refusing to give up even in the face of adversity. In the words of Edward Eggleston, "Persistent people begin their success where others end in failure." *Adaptation* is about shortening the time to success through ingenuity and flexibility. We call this powerful combination *adaptive persistence:* instinctively alternating between anticipation, changing course, and sticking with it, deftly navigating that paradox with aplomb.

When Robert Egger had a vision for feeding the homeless using leftover food from restaurants—while also training them for restaurant and catering jobs—he was greeted by a chorus of naysayers. Only his new bride, Claudia, believed he could do it. He was turned away by everybody—by the caterers, restaurants, foundations, and even the churches that provided homeless services.

"What I found," he says, "is that people, just because they've never seen it, can't believe it. 'Train the homeless?' they'd say. 'I don't think you can do that.'" Still Robert persisted, writing letter after letter to foundations, all to no avail.

After months and months, a letter finally arrived from the Abell Foundation with a check for $25,000. Cash in hand, he bought a refrigerated truck to collect food from restaurants. It was 1988, and George H. W. Bush had just been elected president. With the inauguration and its inaugural balls around the corner, Robert saw an opportunity: massive amounts of unused food and a newly elected U.S. president promoting "a thousand points of light" to encourage community service. This onetime punk rocker cold-called the Republican National Committee and, after days of pestering them, finally struck pay dirt: all of the leftover food from all of the inaugural parties was his if he wanted it.

There he was: massive quantities of food, one truck, no employees. It wasn't his original plan, but he leaped at the chance. "The reason most people fail," he says, "is they're not prepared for success." The day before the inauguration, the *Washington Post* ran a story on his start-up, D.C. Central Kitchen, and then an enterprising local cub reporter named Katie Couric picked up the story, raising awareness about what he was doing. Suddenly, he had more lobster bisque on his hands than he knew what to do with. Against long odds, he spent the night hustling to get the inaugural feast out to shelters across the city, earning a reputation as someone who could deliver on his promise. Before long, Robert's lonely voice was joined by others who understood the vision and the possibilities.

Today, D.C. Central Kitchen serves five thousand meals a day, seven days a week, and just completed its sixty-sixth job training program, now with more than six hundred graduates. Universities across the country have since replicated the Central Kitchen model. As Robert says, "Our job, our only job, is to make the impractical, the improbable, and the impossible possible, plausible, doable."

Adaptive persistence—hanging in through adversity while creatively tailoring one's approach to the circumstances—is a critical skill of the life entrepreneur. Being a life entrepreneur is about proving, again and again, that the impossible is—somehow, someway—possible, plausible, doable. Life entrepreneurs find a way to make things work, no matter the obstacles. "Don't ever let somebody tell you that you can't do something," says Robert. "Never be passive about your life—ever, ever."

Erasing the Lines

Only those who risk going too far can possibly find out how far one can go.
—T. S. Eliot

As T. S. Eliot suggests, in risk we can find profound discovery. Our worlds are confined by imaginary lines. It is the life entrepreneur who is able to erase them, expanding our realm of possibility. "I want to stand as close to the edge as I can without going over," mused Kurt Vonnegut. "Out on the edge you see all the kinds of things you can't see from the center." Erasing the imagined lines around our lives is a dynamic process of envisioning a different reality, summoning the guts to go after it, maintaining the discipline to stick with the effort, and persevering through obstacles.

When Jack Chain was a boy growing up in Delaware, he was determined to qualify for sailing lessons at summer camp. The rule was that no one could take sailing lessons without demonstrating that they could swim fifty feet. Not to be deterred by the small detail that he didn't know how to swim, he jumped off the dock and clawed his way to the shore. Mission accomplished.

Now in his seventies, Chain is a retired four-star general who served with distinction in the United States Air Force for thirty-five years. At a lean six feet, two inches tall, with silver hair, he has a gentle manner that belies an extraordinary career.

In the Reserve Officers Training Corps (ROTC) during college, he wanted to see if he could qualify for pilot training, so he leaped into the cockpit and had a go at it, and his superiors quickly determined that he had the right stuff. After solo flights, he graduated to jets and then fighters.

Eventually, he was flying nuclear-armed F-100 fighter jets over Europe during the frostier days of the cold war, from the Korean War to Vietnam. He found himself in dogfight training with the British and French, flying at five hundred knots fifty feet above ground at 4 g's—four times the accelerating force of the Earth's gravity. Military training standards dictated that his practice strikes land within 1,500 feet of their target; Chain could hit within about 20 feet of his.

In military parlance, he was EWQ: exceptionally well qualified. But it wasn't a fluke. After coasting through much of his youth, he was applying himself for the first time—in situations with life-or-death stakes for himself and others—and thriving under the mantle of that responsibility.

Something unexpected had occurred. The skinny boy from the Delaware suburbs became an intrepid fighter pilot. He accumulated five thousand flying hours, including four hundred in combat, and became a master parachutist. Through it all, he never lost a dogfight, not even in practice. "The guys that really hang it out and fight hard can survive," he says. "It's a real mental switch."

His motivation was simple: *I am responsible.* He sought to do everything to the best of his ability, always working as hard and as long as it took to get the job done—and then some. That meant consistently getting promoted "below the zone" (early and often).

He volunteered to return to Vietnam, assuming a command position and then serving as an instructor with the Aggressors (akin to the navy's "Top Gun" pilot training school). Eventually he was promoted to four-star general and then to commander in chief of the Strategic Air Command (SAC), the major nuclear deterrent force of the United States. He was in the Oval Office weekly, and he oversaw 130,000 people at fifty bases with bombers, tankers, and intercontinental ballistic missiles (ICBMs).

In Jack Chain, we see an ordinary person placed in extraordinary circumstances and rising to the occasion. By assuming responsibility for his life and his comrades, he became "switched on." And by reframing who he was, he was able to serve his country with honor and distinction.

Counterpoint: The Potential Pitfalls of Life Entrepreneurship

Some of the essential traits of an entrepreneur—unfettered optimism, propensity to challenge the status quo, willingness to go it alone, abundant confidence, ambition, tolerance for risk—have potential downsides that can undermine success and sabotage relationships. Here are some of the main pitfalls that sometimes catch entrepreneurs:

- *Ego:* believing the world revolves around us and neglecting to recognize or value the contributions of others, buying into the myth of the heroic lone soldier
- *Lack of focus:* moving from project to project without seeing things through, getting lost in ideas and visions without executing
- *Compulsive drive:* getting lost in work and achievement and losing sight of other priorities, sometimes using people to get what we want
- *Excessive competitiveness:* focusing on winning at all costs, sometimes bending or breaking the rules to prevail
- *Arrogance:* thinking we have all the answers and that we are always right, being blind to our weaknesses
- *Rose-colored glasses:* underestimating challenges through unfounded optimism or naiveté
- *Shortsightedness:* failing to see the big picture and pursuing the latest adrenaline rush while neglecting to build things that last

Of course, none of us is perfect. We all have our flaws, hungers, pitfalls, weaknesses, and hang-ups. But it is essential that we recognize them so we can address them. That requires a strong core identity and healthy relationships with friends and family who are willing to raise red flags when we are on the wrong track. Many of the life entrepreneurs we interviewed were intimately familiar with their personal pitfalls and took active steps to address them. It is possible that knowing what to avoid may be as valuable to entrepreneurs as understanding the entrepreneurial path itself. In the words of Albert Camus, "There is no sun without shadow, and it is essential to know the night."

It's tough for entrepreneurs because I think fundamentally you have to be arrogant to think you can change the world. You just do. So there is definitely some ego involved in thinking you can do things differently. At the same time, paradoxically, if what you care about is getting something done in the world, you must also bring humility to it and recognize that it's not all about you, that there are other people involved. The goal is not self-aggrandizement. The goal is getting this thing you want to do right.

—*Kim Smith, NewSchools Venture Fund*

THE COST OF NOT ACTING

As we seek to avoid mistakes, we should not let that keep us from taking action. Often, the cost of not acting is just too high. Regrettably, that is the price so many of us pay to remain in the realm of safety and comfort.

After college, Seth Goldman entered a "seeking" phase, hoping to reconcile his seemingly disparate interests in public service and entrepreneurship. First, he taught in China for a year—showing up with little more than a backpack—and then cycled through an eclectic parade of jobs: the *Washington Post*, a presidential campaign, teaching English in the former Soviet Union, working on Capitol Hill, and leading the "Summer of Service" program in Baltimore that was a demonstration project for AmeriCorps. It was there, he recalls, that he became "inspired by the notion of creating an organization that could impact the community."

In business school, he spotted an opportunity during a Coke versus Pepsi case study in Professor Barry Nalebuff's class. He saw a gap in the market: Where were the beverages that were flavorful and refreshing but not so sweet?

Years later, after a run in Central Park with a classmate, he couldn't find any drink to quench his thirst that wasn't unnaturally sweetened. Thinking back to business school, he contacted his old professor, Barry, who as it happens had just returned from analyzing the tea industry in India for a case study. Barry even had an idea for a bottled tea made with real tea leaves: "Honest Tea." Seth loved the concept and envisioned a company with "an all-natural brand that would strive to create healthy and honest relationships with its customers, suppliers, and the environment."[4]

At the time, Seth was working for Calvert Group, an investment firm specializing in socially responsible businesses. After conducting research and reaching out to his network for advice, he decided to put his weight behind Honest Tea. "The big moment," he recalls, "was when I went to the president of Calvert and told her I was going to resign to go start this tea company. Before I went up, I called Barry on the phone and said, 'Okay, I'm going to go upstairs and resign. Do you really think we'll be able to make this product?'"

At the time, he and his wife were having their third child. When he was raising money and cashing out his personal investments to fund the start-up, they hadn't even brewed their first batch of tea.

According to Seth, "I said to myself, *You know what? This is the wrong time to do it, but there is never a perfect time. We have the right idea, and I've got to try.*" With his wife's support, he launched Honest Tea out of his guest room and became the "TeaEO." Five weeks later, after brewing countless batches of tea in his kitchen, he brought thermoses (borrowed from Barry) with mock-up labels to Fresh Fields, making a pitch about how there was nothing like this on their shelves. Soon afterward, Fresh Fields ordered fifteen thousand bottles, and Seth was delivering tea bottles—fifty cases at a time—in a U-Haul truck.

This year, Honest Tea will sell about twenty million bottles, making it the best-selling product in its market niche (a beverage category they created). Looking back, Seth says,

> If you don't take some risks early on, it certainly doesn't get any easier. You're in college, you've got loans to pay off, and then you go work for some big, high-paying job and then all of a sudden you move into a fancy apartment and then you've got to pay for that. You buy a fancy car or go to graduate school and you have more loans to pay and all of a sudden you can't take the risk. . . . And then you get married and have kids. We've been living a pretty lean lifestyle. We don't have cable TV. I'm still driving a 1999 Saturn. We try not to get too accustomed to material things that come and go.

By living lean, they were able to jump at the opportunity when it arose.

With his work at Honest Tea, Seth has combined his interests in entrepreneurship and service. "It feels like everything I have done before comes together in running Honest Tea," he says. The company is committed to corporate social responsibility, with initiatives in the environment and innovative partnerships with the tea growers that benefit their communities.

Meanwhile, Seth leads an integrated life. He says, "I make sure that whatever I do, I will create the time and energy to build a meaningful family life and give that top priority. Some of the most rewarding parts of Honest Tea have been when I was able to take my family to the point of origin where we grew our tea. We've been through this Native American community, the Crow Reservation [where Honest Tea partners with the Crow community to be involved in the production and sale of tea]. We've been to India, China, and South Africa where we buy tea. Those experiences are great because they help the whole family appreciate the impact of what we are doing."[5] When asked about what advice he gives to his children, he says, "You're not on Earth for too long, and it's important that you know that what you're doing is of consequence."

This speaks to perhaps the greatest risk of all—the risk of not going for it. This was a resounding theme in our interviews with life entrepreneurs. As we analyze the costs and benefits of embarking on a new venture, we often forget to factor in the cost of regret. As Senator John McCain, a former prisoner of war in Vietnam, writes, "In the past, I've been able to overcome my own fears because of an acute sense of an even greater fear—that of feeling remorse. You can live with pain. You can live with embarrassment. Remorse is an awful companion. And whatever the unwelcome consequences of courage, they are unlikely to be worse than the discovery that you are less than you pretend to be."[6]

The challenges of entrepreneurship are indisputable. It is messy, chaotic, taxing, and risky. Potential failure lurks around many corners. But what is failure, really? Don't we really fail by failing ourselves, our loved ones, and our dreams? We fail by not going for it, not entering the arena, not erasing the lines, and not persevering. If we fall down, we can get up. If we lose our way, we can find our way back. But if we don't summon the courage to take the first step, we will never know where our journey might have taken us.

> One does not discover new lands without consenting
> to lose sight of the shore for a very long time.
> —Andre Gide

CHAPTER NINE

EMBRACING RENEWAL AND REINVENTION

*In life itself, there is a time to seek inner peace,
a time to rid oneself of tension and anxiety. The
moment comes when the striving must let up, when
wisdom says, "Be quiet." You'll be surprised how the
world keeps on revolving without your pushing it.
And you'll be surprised how much stronger you are
the next time you decide to push.*
—JOHN W. GARDNER

During John Gardner's distinguished career, he was secretary of
health, education, and welfare under President Lyndon Johnson,
founder of the prestigious White House Fellows program, president
of the Carnegie Corporation, founder of Common Cause (a non-
profit citizens' lobbying organization), a Marine Corps officer,
board member of several Fortune 500 companies, a faculty member at Stanford University, and a recipient of the Presidential Medal
of Freedom. But it was his love of learning, self-reflection, purposeful action, and ongoing reinvention that made him an exemplar of
life entrepreneurship.

As Gardner once noted, he was "always studying, always trying, always wondering." When he was eighty-eight, he summa-
rized his approach to life in a moving speech, excerpted here:

The luckiest people are those who learn early . . . that it's
essential to take charge of your own life. That doesn't mean

you don't accept help, friendship, love, and leadership—if it's good leadership—from others. But it does mean recognizing that ultimately you're the one who's responsible for you. No excuses. Don't blame others. Don't blame circumstances. You take charge. And one of the things you take charge of is your own learning. . . . Life is an endless unfolding, and if we wish it to be, an endless process of self-discovery, an endless and unpredictable dialogue between our potentialities and the life situations in which we find ourselves.[1]

Life entrepreneurship is about taking charge of our own lives—about pursuing worthy endeavors and maximizing our potential. As Gardner points out, taking charge of our lives is not a onetime action. As we blaze a trail in life, we sometimes lose our way, so we must remain sharply aware of the consequences of our actions, recognize when things are off track, adjust course, and continually learn from our experiences. Often this requires renewal; sometimes it requires reinvention. According to poet Thomas Merton, "Living is the constant adjustment of thought to life and life to thought in such a way that we are always growing, always experiencing new things in the old and old things in the new. Thus life is always new."

Renewal

When Kim Smith helped launch the NewSchools Venture Fund, an innovative venture philanthropy investing in education entrepreneurs, she and her team worked at a breakneck pace. They raised $80 million, scaled quickly, opened up offices on both coasts, created support networks for the leaders they supported, and gathered and disseminated knowledge about how to scale up transformative education enterprises. After seven hard-charging years leading the fund, Kim was burned out.

"The density of my day had become incredible," she recalls. "Fifteen minutes here and fifteen minutes there, a dozen decisions pending, then you have to fly here and then you're flying there, leave that meeting, get in this car, get back on a plane. A lot of people thrive on that. I was just exhausted by it." Her predicament was exacerbated when three of her top executives took a leave of absence at the same time due to personal and health matters. Kim was on overload, and it was affecting her personally as well as her ability to lead at that level.

She began the renewal process through a Crown Fellowship with the Aspen Institute. "Going to Crown got me clear that it was time for me to move on. Part of the Crown experience for me was having real time to reflect and thinking, *That's not the life I want. I can step off that path.*"

After finding her replacement at NSVF, Kim took a yearlong sabbatical. "I took a few months," she says, "to just sit around here seeing my friends and family whom I hadn't seen in a long time, spending time in San Francisco and just recovering. Then I traveled." After exploring Southeast Asia and Africa, she helped to launch the African Leadership Academy, a school focused on developing future generations of African leaders. She explains, "It was back to the creative phase, direct service, and a start-up, which is what I love the best. That really helped recharge my batteries."

Kim is now teaching at Stanford University and hatching several new projects. Most important, she is also finding time for her close relationships. "I want to make a difference," she says, "but I don't have to just sprint on that path the whole time. Now I work from home. My time is much more flexible, and I'm much more relaxed." Through reflection and renewal, she learned a valuable lesson about how to lead her life: "Think about what you're doing," she advises. "Don't just climb the mountain because it's there. Really think about whether that's the mountain you want to climb."

Holding Ourselves Accountable

Did Today Really Matter?
—Sign at the exit of ING Direct USA headquarters[2]

It is all too easy to speed through life with our eyes focused only on the road ahead. The challenge is scanning the horizon from time to time to determine where we are headed. To stay on track, we need to take regular stock of our decisions and actions.

Reflection keeps us focused on the right priorities and account-able to our vision and goals.

To hold ourselves accountable, we should adopt a regular routine of checking progress against our goals, ensuring that our actions reflect our priorities. Do our daily actions have us stuck on an endless treadmill of what Stephen R. Covey calls "high-urgency, low-importance" tasks?[3] Do they have us headed in the wrong direction? How well aligned is our "to do" list with our broader life plan?

Of course, we cannot always follow an orderly list. There are interruptions—unexpected calls, new requests for help, fires to put out. It helps to set regular check-in times. Many people use the morning to make a list of the day's activities. Why not take time to assess how this list stacks up against our longer-term pri-orities? At the middle and end of the day, we can then pause to take stock and make adjustments.

Building in such reflection time also provides opportunities to celebrate accomplishments. By savoring the simple joys of the day—a great sunrise, an invigorating workout, a catch-up con-versation with a friend, story time with a child, a breakthrough at work—we put ourselves in a positive frame of mind. This becomes habitual and can lead to a string of good decisions and actions—two key components of a life well spent.

The Consequences of Overload

When we are charging into a new enterprise, relationship, or com-mitment, we want to give it our all. As we do so, pressure increases, and we are tempted to drive faster and harder. Although some stress can actually increase performance, too much can lead to burnout and decreased output. A century ago two Harvard doctors, Robert Yerkes and John Dodson, developed a stress and perfor-mance model that is still highly relevant (if not more so) today. As Figure 9.1 shows, there is a tipping point where stress detracts from performance.[4]

Stress is no stranger to the life entrepreneur—we drive our-selves hard. But maintaining that pace over the long haul with-out deteriorating performance is tough. Stress accumulates over time, sometimes with devastating effects on our health.

FIGURE 9.1. STRESS AND PERFORMANCE.

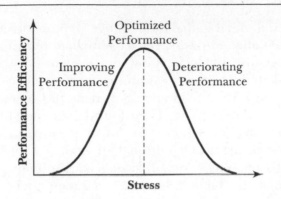

Gerald Chertavian got a wake-up call one night at the office:

I looked over the side of my desk in London. It was two AM
and I couldn't see the ground. It was just black. I couldn't even
see the rug below me. It was like looking into the abyss. Right
there, I realized that I wasn't doing what I needed to do with my
life. Then I went home and gave myself grades as a father, husband,
friend, community member, and business person, and I only got
one A and the A was as a business person. I said that's the last
time in my life I'm going to look in the mirror and give myself
those grades, period.

There are several leading stress inducers: overcommitting
ourselves and not being able to fulfill our promises, intense time
pressures (including a debilitating sense of too many things to do
and not enough hours in the day), being subject to matters outside of our control, and high-stakes decisions clouded by insufficient information. When we tip over into high-stress mode, we
immediately feel the impact: anger, frustration, irritability, poor
judgment, lack of focus, and diminished creativity—reducing our
enjoyment as well as our productivity. As Edward Hallowell writes
in *Crazy Busy*, "Being too busy, which can seem necessary and
unavoidable, can become a habit so entrenched that it leads you
to postpone or cut short what really matters to you, making you a
slave to a lifestyle you don't like but you can't escape. You can be
so busy that you don't even take the time to decide what actually
does matter the most to you, let alone make the time to do it."[5]

DAILY RENEWAL

Daily renewal rituals—the little things we can do each day to restore our sanity and perspective—enhance our ability to handle the pressure. Exploring how performance levels could be maintained in high-stress conditions, performance consultants Jim Loehr and Tony Schwartz looked at the behavior of tennis and golf professionals. They found that high-performance athletes are able to achieve an "ideal performance state" by increasing their physical, emotional, mental, and spiritual capacities through ongoing renewal strategies. Although pro athletes must train at the highest levels to maintain their competitive advantage, their workouts can be stressful and even painful.

The key to reaping the benefits of these workouts and avoiding chronic injury and burnout is the recovery process. As Loehr and Schwartz write, "The enemy is not stress, it's linearity—the failure to oscillate between energy expenditure and recovery." For this, they advocate "precise recovery rituals." For instance, they showed that pro tennis players who took time between points to refocus, lower their heart rate, shake off any negative feelings, and visualize the next point were far less likely to choke under pressure. Jack Nicklaus once wrote in *Golf Digest,* "I've developed a regimen that allows me to move from peaks of concentration into valleys of relaxation and back again as necessary. My focus begins to sharpen as I walk back onto the tee and steadily intensifies . . . until I hit [my drive]. . . . I descend into a valley as I leave the tee."[6]

Athletes who fail to adopt the right mind-set face the consequences. Anxiety and fear undermine confidence; anger and frustration easily distract. Moreover, if these feelings remain, stress levels can increase, leading to a vicious cycle. Like professional athletes, we all can increase our performance by consistently building in time for recovery.

These findings resonate with other research on brain functioning and performance. Our productivity and sense of well-being are highly dependent on our health. Among the most recommended strategies for increasing productivity and reducing stress are regular exercise, healthy diet, quick mental breaks, adequate sleep, kicking bad habits, and recharging every ninety minutes.[7] To that list, we would add meditation, creative departures from the usual routines, and otherwise finding ways to "get out of our head" on a regular basis. When we relax, high-stress problems are placed in perspective. The mental shift also allows the more creative and intuitive right brain to take over from the logic-oriented left brain.

According to Suzanne McKechnie Klahr of BUILD, "I come up with the answers to some of my toughest problems when I'm swimming laps." Thomas Jefferson reportedly believed in getting two hours of exercise a day, and Thomas Edison, Winston Churchill, and Ronald Reagan were all nappers.[8] A recent study of twenty-three thousand adults in Greece showed that those who regularly napped had a 37 percent lower risk of dying from a heart attack than those who did not.[9]

We ignore the basics of our physical, mental, emotional, and spiritual well-being at our own peril. It is helpful to have a sanctuary—a place of refuge or joyful activity where we can find peace and quiet for deep reflection, whether through prayer, meditation, yoga, hiking in the woods, jogging on a deserted road, reading a novel, listening to music, or whatever else brings us that reprieve.

It's important to make daily renewal a cherished habit. Busy weekends and rare vacations are not enough to keep our battery charged, especially if we are sneaking in work on the weekends. Rob Glaser of RealNetworks says that the most powerful source of daily renewal for him "is when I go home and hang out with my babies. I look at that curious, expansive, and excited look on the faces of our seven-month-old son and daughter, and wow." That "wow" moment, however it arrives, is what keeps our head up and clears our mind for the road ahead.

LONGER-TERM RENEWAL

> *The afternoon knows what the morning never suspected.*
> —SWEDISH PROVERB

Despite our best efforts to stay on track through daily renewal, life conspires against predictability and linearity. Whether due to changing circumstances, unexpected disruptions, or burnout, we tend to travel through cycles in life. Tuning in to these rhythms is part of the longer-term renewal process.

We cannot stay in action mode forever (a lesson that is hard for many entrepreneurs to learn). Being a "captain" requires both high drive and direction, but periodically we need to pull over, take a breath, consult the map, and get our bearings. Sometimes we need to seek or drift. Easing back occasionally helps keep the joyful entrepreneurial spirit alive.

Two years into his presidency, Teddy Roosevelt—a quintessential life entrepreneur—wrote to the naturalist and ardent conservationist, John Muir, asking him to serve as a guide for a trip to Yosemite in California. Muir agreed, and in May 1903 the two men set out to explore the Sierra Nevada mountains with some pack mules. When they returned, Roosevelt was refreshed and brimming with resolve. He announced, "I have just come from four days' rest in Yosemite. . . . Lying out at night under those giant sequoias was lying in a temple built by no hand of man, a temple grander than any human architect could by any possibility build, and I hope for the preservation of the groves of giant trees simply because it would be a shame to our civilization to let them disappear."

Roosevelt went on to establish the U.S. Forest Service and by the end of his presidency had set aside 194 million acres for nature preserves and national parks, including the Yosemite Valley. Muir himself remained an outspoken conservationist, including cofounding and leading the Sierra Club, and was constantly sharpening his saw by staying close to his muse: "I only went out for a walk and finally concluded to stay out till sundown, for going out, I found, was really going in."[10]

> There is one means of procuring solitude which to
> me, and I apprehend all men, is effectual, and that
> is to go to a window and look at the stars. If they do
> not startle you and call you off from vulgar matters,
> I know not what will.
> —RALPH WALDO EMERSON

Taking the time for restoration can help us spend more time in the "captain's chair" over our lifetime. The alternative is pushing so hard that we risk losing our drive and direction.

Several of the life entrepreneurs we interviewed became "trapped by success" at various points in their lives, which made it harder for them to make the changes they wanted to make. Business school professors Donald Sull and Dominic Houlder call this "active inertia." When we are moving full throttle toward achieving our goals, a number of the components that led to success actually inhibit us from future success. As Sull and Houlder comment, "The ruts that lock people into active inertia are the very commitments that led to their past successes but that have now hardened: strategic frames become blinders, selected processes lapse into routines, relationships turn into shackles, resources become millstones, and once vibrant values ossify into dogmas. . . . The force of inertia is every bit as powerful in our personal lives as it is in most organizations."[11]

How can we avoid these traps? Author Richard Leider suggests that at critical junctures in our lives we do a full-fledged "life review"—including home and family, work, relationships, health, and spirit—including a "vocational inventory" to determine whether we are using our strengths and making contributions through our work.[12] Sometimes these life reviews call for taking a time-out to reflect, reevaluate, and change direction.

Pulling over when we are barreling down the autobahn of life requires discipline and a willingness to accept some professional risk. We convince ourselves that we will lose the race if we pull into a pit stop to refuel. That, of course, assumes that life is a race. "The trouble with the rat race," quips Lily Tomlin, "is that even if you win, you're still the rat."

Sometimes we are aided in our renewal efforts by forward-thinking organizations. The card company Hallmark is just such a place. Keeping the creative juices flowing is mission critical for Hallmark. To support its roughly eight hundred artists, designers, and writers producing over nineteen thousand new greeting card designs every year, the company has built a 180,000-square-foot "innovation facility" next to its headquarters to facilitate creative renewal. The building is packed with a wide variety of craft studios: bead making, ceramics, leather tooling, and more. It also has a nearby farm where employees can learn woodworking and blacksmithing. All employees are periodically encouraged to take a four- to six-month rotation in these creative hotboxes.

These mechanisms of creative renewal are a form of artistic cross-training.[13] And Hallmark is not alone. Increasing numbers of organizations are now offering periodic sabbaticals to help people stay fresh over the long haul.[14]

CYCLES OF RENEWAL

Many people "get" renewal intellectually but have a hard time actually engaging in it regularly. In this section, we provide a brief road map for renewal based on our interviews and research. The renewal process cycles through four stages: awakening, reflection, planning, and action (see Figure 9.2).

FIGURE 9.2. HEALTHY CYCLES OF RENEWAL.

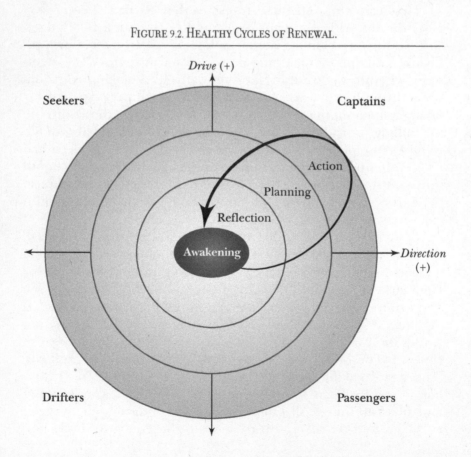

STAGE I. AWAKENING

The first stage of renewal is *awakening*, when we begin to consider the possibility of change, the possibility that all is not right. Think back to Kimberly Wilson, whose awakening led her to start a yoga studio to create the life she desired.

Awakenings can happen any time. Karin Weber had an awakening when she turned sixty. She had been a teacher, real estate and stock broker, sales manager, executive at Merrill Lynch, and trustee of many non-profit boards. She and her husband, Bob, had a beautiful home at the top of a wind-swept Colorado mountain. They had two healthy and active children. Karin had traveled around the world, was active in her community, had terrific friends, and had consistently advanced professionally.

But those years of success left her feeling empty. She recalls, "I lost a lot of time and wasted a lot of energy by running after achievements to validate myself. It was all about how many things I could have on my résumé. It was like living on junk food. I was never living according to my own life vision but rather trying to live up to others' expectations of me."

Part of her challenge was balancing the demands of the workplace with the demands of motherhood. She explains,

> These pressures, when you have children and dual careers and you're trying to do everything, are just exhausting. One time we went on a family vacation and they were all out on the beach, but I just slept all day. . . . I loved being a young mother, but I worried that life was passing me by and that I'd never have a chance to get into the workplace. I wanted to have it all, but I felt a constant tension. When I combined being a wife and mother with a career, the tension remained but in a different guise. Wherever I was, whether at home or work, I felt like I should be spending more time at the other place.

At sixty, Karin embarked on a new path. At the urging of her mentor, she traveled to Santa Monica, California, to study spiritual psychology. That awakened a part of her that had long slumbered, and it renewed her passion for life. She is now pursuing her Ph.D., writing books, caring for dying patients in hospice, and helping to launch camps for children with cancer. She reflects,

"I am grateful to have learned from these challenges and mistakes because it is through them that I now understand myself better. It took me sixty years to trust myself."

STAGE II. REFLECTION

The second stage of renewal is *reflection,* in which we revisit our core identity and cycle back to what is important in our lives. This requires both sanctuary and time to let it unfold.

Randy Komisar has found great power in reflection. He ranged through a wide gamut of professions before landing on what made his heart sing. Over the course of twenty-five years he worked for eleven companies in what he calls a "crazy quilt" of jobs, including community development manager, music promoter, corporate lawyer, technology start-up CFO, and CEO of several dynamic companies. He left a promising career track at a law firm to join Apple in the early Macintosh days (cofounding Claris Corporation), served as CEO of LucasArts Entertainment (with George Lucas, the visionary behind the "Star Wars" franchise), and saw his career get on "the CEO track."

Though the CEO track was challenging, respectable, and lucrative, Randy wanted to ensure that he was the captain of his life. "In the way that I define success," he says, "there's only one way to be successful and that is to love what you do and to be passionate about the purpose and meaning that you're engaged with. . . . Ultimately, the risk I'm afraid of taking is the risk of a life unlived, of not living up to my values and having some sense of purpose and fulfillment in what I'm doing."

After a healthy reflection process, he chose to create his own destiny and become a "virtual CEO," which allows him to do what he loves and does best: creating environments in which people can be creative, stretch themselves, grow, work together as teams, and have an impact on society.

For Randy, reflection is an essential part of what he calls "a considered life." He explains,

> If you pay attention, if you ask yourself the questions about life, satisfaction, fulfillment, and purpose, that process becomes constant and never-ending. It is simple to say but very hard to do. Very

few people I know pay a lot of attention to these core elements of purpose, mission, principles, and values. They give it some thought, but they get carried away by the trajectory of the life expectations that have been in part created for them. . . . It all starts by paying attention and constantly reexamining and potentially resetting that compass. Basically, the real question is: *What are you willing to do for the rest of your life?*

Within the renewal cycle, it is important to ensure that the reflection stage lasts long enough to recharge our batteries and give us new bearings, but without extending into hibernation. Then we are ready to transition to the planning stage.

STAGE III. PLANNING

Planning is the staging ground for taking action anew. After reflection, we need to gather our thoughts and map out a plan for how to proceed. This requires setting goals, developing a smart strategy for proceeding, and initiating low-risk experiments. As we plan, we must avoid the trap of analysis paralysis as we try to devise the perfect sequence of next steps. (Recall Herminia Ibarra's counterintuitive findings about successful career changes in Chapter Six.) Sometimes the best way to plan is to start taking action in thoughtful ways to get us moving and help us discern the way forward.

STAGE IV. ACTION

Once we have cycled through the awakening, reflection, and planning stages, it is time for full-fledged action. As we covered the dynamics of taking action in the previous chapter, here we will only emphasize that breaking old patterns of behavior is difficult. But renewal is rarely about starting over; rather, it usually means building from what we know and love to do—as well as what we want to avoid. With each new chapter of our life, we gain a clearer sense of who we are, where we want to go, and how we can best get there.

The cycles of renewal may look straightforward on paper, but in reality they are rarely so. Only with time can we achieve clarity.

And though renewal is usually something we choose to initiate when it is needed, sometimes it is initiated for us in life through adversity.

"CRUCIBLES"

The world breaks everyone, and afterward, many are strong at the broken places.
—ERNEST HEMINGWAY

In their study of generational leadership for the book, *Geeks and Geezers: How Era, Values, and Defining Moments Shape Leaders,* Warren Bennis and Robert Thomas found a common factor in all the leaders they profiled: a positive and productive response to an intense, transformative experience. They called these "crucibles," named after the vessel in which medieval alchemists attempted to turn base metals into gold. They write, "Whether imposed or not, crucibles are places where essential questions are asked: Who am I? Who could I be? Who should I be?"[15] Nelson Mandela's crucible was twenty-nine years in prison. "If I had not been in prison," he explained in an interview in 2001, "I would not have been able to achieve the most difficult task in life, that is, changing yourself." Crucibles test our mettle. If we survive them, we may emerge stronger.

Austrian psychiatrist Victor Frankl was a World War II prisoner for over two and a half years in several Nazi concentration camps, including Auschwitz. His wife, father, mother, and brother—his entire family save for his sister—died in camps. Yet remarkably, he not only survived but also developed an entire philosophy from his experiences with the Holocaust, centered on "man's search for meaning." Frankl took solace in his ability to attend to the physical and psychological well-being of his fellow prisoners, and he found motivation in his desire to catalog the "tragic optimism" that could be found even in hell on Earth. He says, "It is a peculiarity of man that he can only live by looking to the future. . . . The prisoner who had lost faith in the future—his future—was doomed."[16]

He observed that some prisoners at the camps managed to survive better than others by taking refuge in a life of "inner riches" and "spiritual freedom." "Everything can be taken from a man," he wrote, "but one thing: the last of the human freedoms—to choose one's attitude in any given set of circumstances, to choose one's own way. . . . It is this spiritual freedom—which cannot be taken away—that makes life meaningful and purposeful."[17]

Frankl shows how redemption can be born even from tragedy—through our ability to choose how we respond to it.

On a trip through Mexico before business school, David Carmel dove into the surf and hit a sandbar, breaking his neck. "Not being able to move below the chest forced me to sit with hard feelings," he recounts. "I went from being as independent as you can possibly imagine to lying in a hospital bed and having people to do everything for me. My immediate reaction was coping. I had been a big goal setter, but that all shrank to addressing basic needs that I had learned when I was three years old."

This was especially difficult for a young man who had been active all his life, from wrestling and singing to volunteering in high school at a drug treatment center and then a tutoring program. After college, he had cofounded Jumpstart, a non-profit organization (built from ideas and research from his college senior thesis) that connects college students with disadvantaged youth to assist them with basic skill building. He recalls, "It was the first time I had the chance to mobilize the resources around me to try to make an idea happen. I can't think of anything more satisfying."

After his accident, David drew heavily on his own resolve and the support of others to keep moving forward. A year later, he reenrolled at business school and then earned a White House Fellowship. Today he is an executive at a stem cell blood bank company called StemCyte and advises top state officials on stem cell policy. It was his way of turning a personal crisis into an opportunity. "In some ways," he says, "my spinal cord injury got me reengaged in my science interests. Dealing with rehab and understanding how my body worked got me very excited about the medical field. It was definitely a life circumstance that was the impetus, but in many ways it was reconnecting with a passion."

David was recently married, literally sweeping his bride, Kirsten, off her feet during their first dance, and he credits the support he received during his darkest hours as being essential.

Through his crucible, David found the fortitude not only to survive and cope but also to grow and serve. "A lot of people have sacrificed on my behalf," he acknowledges. "Since I have had to battle back, it's given me a lot of confidence in my ability to do something much grander in the future. It's powerful to show that you can pursue something with the same intensity as you could before."

REINVENTION

Sometimes renewal is not enough and life demands reinvention. Often this occurs after a time of adversity, such as a medical emergency or divorce, or during what has been called our "second half"—a midlife transition, retirement, or another realization that big changes are needed.

Examples of personal reinvention abound. Consider what Betty Ford did with her life after battling addiction—not to mention Jimmy Carter and Bill Clinton after their presidencies, Ronald Reagan after his acting career, and Al Gore's transition into environmental advocacy. Consider Paul Newman's transition from acting to charitable work or Clint Eastwood's transition from "Dirty Harry" movies to politics and elegant film directing. Then there's U2's Bono, who went from rock star to global humanitarian. For some of us, real living doesn't begin until we reorient our priorities and reinvent our lives.

The day after graduating from college, Billy Shore drove to Washington, D.C., and knocked on the door of Colorado senator Gary Hart. He was intrigued by the maverick senator who had earned a reputation of supporting what he believed was best for the country regardless of political expediency. For Billy, government service was his chance to make a difference.

Years later, Shore found himself decompressing after an intense presidential campaign in which Senator Hart lost the Democratic nomination to Walter Mondale. It gave him a chance to "breathe deeply and read expansively" and figure out his next move. "For the last three years," he recalls, "I had stood behind the curtain listening to Senator Hart give the same speech fifty times the same week. I started thinking, *Well, what about some of the things that I care about?*"

At the time, the Ethiopian famine was headlining the daily newspaper stories. "What was happening in Ethiopia really hit me," he recalls. "It captured my imagination." There were prominent efforts to address it, including LiveAid, but Billy noticed that all of them were designed to make a splash yet none was designed to endure.

With his sister, Debbie, he started a non-profit organization, Share Our Strength, focused on famine relief. For the next three years, the organization limped along as Shore juggled leading the small non-profit and serving as Hart's campaign manager for the upcoming presidential election.

Shortly after Hart announced his candidacy, his campaign blew up in a scandal. Billy recalls, "There are campaigns that you lose, but his ended abruptly with about six hours' notice. We had sold our house in D.C. and taken an eighteen-month lease in Colorado for a campaign that lasted twenty-one days from announcement to withdrawal. I was shell-shocked and terribly disappointed. I wasn't going to be doing what I had been training to do for the last decade."

As he wondered whether his career was over, he spotted an opportunity for personal reinvention. He explains, "I didn't get involved in the Hart campaign because I wanted to work in the White House, but because I really wanted to be involved with his ideas. Then I realized I could advance these ideas in other ways."

He returned to the Share Our Strength office forty-eight hours later with a renewed commitment and threw himself into its mission-driven work. Through innovative revenue-generating strategies, such as a strategic partnership with American Express, the organization has since raised more than $200 million to support more than a thousand antihunger and antipoverty groups worldwide, has become the leading organization working to end childhood hunger in the United States, and has spun off an innovative for-profit subsidiary called Community Wealth Ventures.

In the process, Shore not only reinvented his own life dramatically but also got to work on reinventing the way non-profits approach their resources and work. He has since become a leading advocate worldwide for how non-profits can partner with for-profit companies in mutually beneficial ways that generate community wealth—not just "teaching men how to fish," as he says, "but teaching them how to build fisheries."

Shore's recipe for personal reinvention is powerful: "What I've come to trust is the impulse inside that is very strong, that when I see or hear something that really affects me, I try to pay a lot of attention to it. That usually sets me up in some unexpected direction. . . . I urge people not to go through life getting their ticket punched so they can later go do what they want to do. I think you should try to do what you want to do right away. The best way is to just start doing it."

LEADING AN INTEGRATED LIFE

To thine own self be true.
—POLONIUS IN WILLIAM SHAKESPEARE'S *HAMLET*

The benefits of renewal and reinvention, beyond resting and recharging, often include restoring authenticity and passion to our lives. Being true to ourselves requires aligning each of the components in our life with our core identity and with the direction in which we want to travel. When we drive too hard or end up on the wrong path, we must have the courage to stop, look around, and self-correct. Renewal and reinvention help keep us on track.

This is not a one-dimensional task affecting only single strands of life. As we renew and reinvent, we must address our lives as a whole, bringing all the strands together, including personal, professional, relational, spiritual, and other dimensions that matter to us. As we strive to piece together this dynamic puzzle, our aim should be a life of congruence, one in which the different elements agree with one another in ways that cohere. Congruence entails living in dynamic harmony, where the strands of our lives play in concert together in a way that has deep and meaningful resonance—and that changes as we learn and grow.

Most people think about this in terms of maintaining "balance" in their lives—ensuring enough time for each of the important elements that they value. But time is just one variable (albeit an important one) and doesn't speak to the quality and nature of our respective endeavors. What's more, such thinking allows us to compartmentalize these endeavors without having the disparate elements cohere.

Randy Komisar has thought long and hard about this, both for himself and for the emerging leaders he mentors. He says, "My life is integral. What I do, who I am, what I believe, is one integrated life. As you look around the workplace today, the banter around balanced life is misdirected. It's really about alignment, integration, and the notion of building some flexibility and control into how the work is done. . . . I think what they're asking for is the opportunity to do meaningful, challenging work where they can grow and create, and to be able to have sufficient control in their lives to integrate all the other things in a dynamic way."

Best-selling author Mark Albion makes the case that the only way for us to achieve balance is to make our passion and our work one and the same.[18] We speak of this as *leading an integrated life*. We can't just shut off our work self when we walk in the door in the evening or shut off our private self when we stroll into the office or job site; nor should we. Our values and purpose should resonate with every aspect of our life, showing up in all of our activities. Author Bill George (*True North*) is clear on this point: "You can be the same person in every aspect of your life, in your personal life, your spiritual life, in your work, in your home, family life, and in your community. When we don't have that congruence, eventually it is going to blow up."

Every day we have decisions to make about how we want to live. To achieve our "potentialities," as Gardner calls them, we must take charge of how we spend our days. As we live and learn through action and experience, we must also grow through renewal and, sometimes, reinvention. Otherwise, we may one day wake up to find ourselves brilliantly situated for a life we do not want.

CONCLUSION: CREATING A NEW FUTURE

*The great affair, the love affair with life, is to live as
variously as possible, to groom one's curiosity like a
high-spirited thoroughbred, climb aboard, and gallop
over the thick, sun-struck hills every day. Where
there is no risk, the emotional terrain is flat and
unyielding, and, despite all its dimensions, valleys,
pinnacles, and detours, life will seem to have none
of its magnificent geography, only a length. It began
in mystery, and it will end in mystery, but what a
savage and beautiful country lies in between.*
—DIANE ACKERMAN, *A NATURAL HISTORY OF THE SENSES*[1]

Who do I want to be?
What is life asking of me?
How do I want to live?
What future do I want to create?

Through fifty-five telling stories, we have seen how others
have begun to answer these questions. Each chose a different
path, but all elected to "gallop over the thick, sun-struck hills."
All took responsibility for their lives and made choices based
on a deep understanding of who they are. Each has weathered
challenges and experienced the "savage" country, yet all have witnessed the beauty that appears when we take risks and yield to
the great love affair with life.

And they are all having an effect on the world around them.
This effect is not limited to the concentric rings that ripple out
from their actions. Rather, these life entrepreneurs are harbingers of changing times, signaling important shifts in the way rising

165

generations are thinking about and leading their lives. By studying the stories and choices of life entrepreneurs, we not only learn more about our path in life, but we also can begin to understand the priorities and decisions of emerging generations born of an entrepreneurial age.

In these final pages, we explore three overarching societal trends that emerged through our research and interviews. We believe these trends have direct implications for our future—from our workplaces and schools to our communities, social frameworks, and life priorities. Life entrepreneurs are pioneers who are helping to create these trends, pushing forward from the front lines. These overarching trends are a departure from fashions of old and are playing out everywhere we look. Accordingly, once we lay out these trends and their implications, we return to storytelling. In two concluding stories, we introduce a trio of life entrepreneurs who embody these overarching trends and are helping to lead a galloping charge toward a sun-struck future.

TRENDS OF THE ENTREPRENEURIAL AGE

Generations are shaped by defining moments—from World War II, the Vietnam War, and the countercultural movements of the 1960s in the United States to the Cultural Revolution in China, the fall of the Berlin Wall in Europe, and the anti-apartheid movement in South Africa. Today's rising generations have come of age during a boom in entrepreneurship and are helping shape the future through their organizations and disruptive innovations. Think Google, YouTube, Skype, Facebook, wireless communications, open source collaboration, instant messaging, microlending, file sharing, bioengineering, nanotechnology, and more. Consider the following:

- "At any given time," according to Carl Schramm, president of the Ewing Marion Kauffman Foundation, "15 percent of the [U.S.] population is running their own companies. . . . These entrepreneurs, people who now create more than half the new jobs in America, are defining the new economy not just here but around the world. . . . We now live in the most entrepreneurial time in history. In fact, we could call the current era the age of entrepreneurial capitalism. We have entered a time of continuous innovation."[2]

- According to the Global Entrepreneurship Monitor Report 2002, 50 percent of global entrepreneurial activity is accounted for by men and women between ages twenty-five and forty-four.[3]
- According to the massive 2002 Panel Study of Entrepreneurial Dynamics, "the creation of a new firm is more widespread than the creation of a new household or the birth of a baby."[4]
- About 465,000 new businesses are created each month in the United States, according to estimates from the *Kauffman Index of Entrepreneurial Activity, 1996–2006.*[5]
- According to the Entrepreneurial Research Consortium, "Some 37 percent of U.S. households include someone who has founded, tried to start, or helped fund a small business."[6]
- According to the Global Entrepreneurship Monitor Report 2005, "More than 30 million women world-wide are entrepreneurs, accounting for 41 percent of a total 73 million people involved in starting up a business in 2004."[7]

As entrepreneurship has expanded in our global economy, it has also seeped into our lives, pervading our attitudes and approaches. We are entering into an age in which personal priorities, collective values, and societal boundaries are shifting. The fifty-five people we interviewed are not only exemplars of life entrepreneurship but also pioneers of living in this age. In classic entrepreneurial fashion, they are altering the status quo and driving changes in the way we work, learn, and live.

UNTETHERING

The first overarching trend is what we call *untethering*—breaking away from traditional institutions and structures while coalescing into increasingly virtual configurations and connections, shedding the ties that have bound us. We see this in the shift from highly structured, full-service corporations to a greater prevalence of dynamic free agents and specialized providers of products and services. People are untethering from traditional careers and opting instead for discrete sets of work activities and periodic professional reinventions. According to the U.S. Bureau of Labor Statistics, the median tenure for employed wage and salary workers is just four years, and 23 percent of them have been with their current employer for twelve months or less. Today, people are shunning centralized work centers and gravitating toward flexible, virtual productivity in a range of unlikely places. Work is becoming unhitched from the standard workweek of Monday through Friday, nine to five. It is being blown out into "bursts of time" that are productivity and outcome based, not time standardized. Think back to Stacey Boyd's Savvy Source for Parents: the company's data on U.S. preschools is gathered by working mothers across the country who are coordinating their work and family time in flexible arrangements, thereby freeing up their lives.

In education, we are increasingly moving away from "one size fits all" large schools and beginning to embrace smaller learning communities focused on individual learning needs. People are learning on their own time in their own ways, and entrepreneurs are creating new learning environments to meet this demand. We see this with the rise of virtual schools (in which students can study anytime and anywhere, assisted by online instruction and tutoring) as well as courses and learning modules catering to discrete and disparate needs and interests. We are unpacking the traditional schooling environment through innovative instructional practices and multimedia technology so that learning is no longer associated with rows of children staring at a blackboard. In the best classrooms, student learning is becoming more individualized—identifying students' strengths and weaknesses, catering to their learning interests and skills, and allowing them to develop skill sets that will help them navigate a future of dynamic change and uncertainty.

In our communities, we are untethering from local neighborhoods as the focal point of our social lives. Those physical communities are now being supplemented by distributed networks based on shared interests and values. This trend is being facilitated by technology and increased mobility. We see this in emerging connections among the cultural creatives and in networks of free agents.

It is worth noting that the increasing prevalence of free agents carries the danger of creating a toxic hyperindividualism and disconnected physical communities. How can communities be structured to embrace entrepreneurial living in ways that bind us together instead of driving us apart? It is an open question, but we see early responses in the "new" urbanism—with careful attention to creating holistic and sustainable living communities with vibrant social hubs—and new forms of architecture and design that promote gathering spaces.

Additionally, many in the rising generations are drifting away from affiliations with organized religion and its traditions and institutions and gravitating to more personalized approaches to the divine, from meditation and yoga to encountering spirituality in nature. Kimberly Wilson's Tranquil Space in Washington, D.C., is an example of how new kinds of like-minded communities are emerging that blend ancient practices (such as yoga) with more modern sensibilities.

The result of all this untethering is a growing number of lives that are more free-flowing and uniquely designed by each person, no longer tied to traditional modes of living or career paths. Today, more and more people are making conscious, courageous decisions to blaze their own trail in life. They are forgoing an existence defined by safety, security, and status, instead choosing lives infused with passion, connection, and significance (products of the second trend, which we now explore).

AUTHENTICITY

The second overarching trend is *authenticity*—finding a fit between how we appear in the world (especially through work and family) and our genuine selves (particularly our passions and values). Rising generations are tired of losing themselves in busyness and putting in ungodly hours at workplaces that define them by the narrow confines of a job description instead of recognizing their humanity, distinctive gifts, and interest in community contribution. They are looking for workplaces that value them as individuals, with their unique ideas, talents, skills, and interests. Consider this: in a recent study in the United Kingdom, "nearly nine out of ten young people are seeking careers that would 'add purpose to their lives as well as fulfill their potential at work,' 59 percent feel that their current job 'doesn't fulfill' their 'wider life ambitions,' and 50 percent feel that their employers 'do not care about them as individuals.'"[8]

Conversely, the kind of workplace that they yearn for is being created by Gary Erickson and his wife Kit at Clif Bar. By walking the walk of environmental sustainability (through their green initiatives), creativity and fun (through their theater space and jam sessions), physical health (through their gym and wellness programs), community engagement (through their voluntarism and philanthropy), and work-life balance (through their three-day weekend program), they are creating opportunities for people to manifest their authentic values every day through their work—all while making a good living for their families.

There is a hunger today for work infused with purpose. It is no longer enough to work for a paycheck; there is a growing belief that a good life requires work in pursuit of something meaningful and lasting, including creating quality and value, serving, and problem solving—especially in the face of the significant environmental, economic, political, and diplomatic challenges that rising generations have inherited.

The rise of social entrepreneurship, in which people are creating dynamic non-profit enterprises focused on positive social transformation, is a leading indicator of this trend. Clear examples of this are the creation of organizations such as Suzanne McKechnie Klahr's BUILD, Robert Egger's D.C. Central Kitchen, Jael Kampfe's Four Times Foundation, and Raj Vinnakota and Eric Adler's SEED Foundation (and school). This trend is also evident in the conscientious consumer choices people are making, as they use them to send signals about their concerns and values.

Learning institutions are starting to pay closer attention to individual student needs and interests. As part of this trend, we expect that individual lifelong learning plans will be developed, maintained, and updated throughout our lives. Students are being asked to play a greater role in their own learning, helping to choose their schools and educational programs and set their own learning goals. More and more schools are recognizing opportunities to expose students early on to "awakening" and character-forming opportunities, such as global travel, outdoor education, team- and project-based learning, entrepreneurship education, voluntary service learning, internships, and more. Additionally, American students are following a growing

European trend of taking a "gap" year between high school and college—facilitated by organizations such as Interim Programs in Cambridge, Massachusetts.[9] As a result, students can develop a better sense of who they are and where they want to go. Mike Feinberg and David Levin's Knowledge Is Power Program (KIPP) places this kind of character-based education at the forefront of its powerful strategy for transforming the lives of underserved urban youth, with phenomenal results.

Finally, people are increasingly making their choice of where to live based on their values and priorities.[10] For life entrepreneurs, finding a home that resonates with their values, interests, and needs is important. Just look at Stacey Boyd and Scott Hamilton's decision to move to Jackson Hole, Wyoming, now instead of waiting until retirement. Jael Kampfe decided to return to her family's ranch in Montana because that is where her roots are. Howard Schultz pursued an opportunity at Starbucks in part because he was smitten with Seattle, and Max Israel lives there so he can get twenty-five days of "secret office" time in the mountains of the Pacific Northwest. Mayor Hickenlooper of Denver, a geologist turned brewpub entrepreneur, is developing a city that attracts cultural creatives and business, social, and life entrepreneurs by investing in infrastructure—such as mass transit, bike lanes, and communal work and social spaces—that reflects emerging priorities, values, and sensibilities.

INTEGRATION

Integration—a restoration of coherence and congruence in our lives—is the third overarching trend of the entrepreneurial age. Rising generations are eager to address the unhealthy disconnect that comes from compartmentalizing our work and personal lives. People work with a different blend of motivations today: less emphasis on income and security and more on learning, challenge, fun, fulfillment, and service. This means looking for work that provides opportunities to contribute value and pay the bills while also allowing for robust outside pursuits, including time for family, health and wellness, adventure, travel, enjoyment, learning, spirituality, and more. Life entrepreneurs recognize that this often requires difficult trade-offs, but they are willing to do what it takes to preserve their integrated approach. For instance, Seth Goldman and his wife live modestly in order to provide their family with maximum flexibility to pursue new opportunities like the one that led to the creation of Honest Tea. Beth and Devon Santa downsized their material footprint on land to fund their entrepreneurial adventures at sea.

Forward-thinking organizations are embracing this integrated lifestyle by investing more in the health, education, and well-being of people who work with and for them. Larry Leith at Tokyo Joe's, for instance, measures his success based on the exceptional care and opportunities the company provides to its employees—"the few, the proud, the pierced." Likewise, the ability to provide employees with a creative place to work and play is a major talent attraction differentiator for Richard Tait's board game company Cranium.

Integration can also be seen in the blurring of our sectors. Organizations like Billy Shore's Share Our Strength and Kim Smith's NewSchools Venture Fund are applying for-profit principles and practices to non-profit organizations. Likewise, companies like Gun Denhart's Hanna Andersson and Linda Mason and Roger Brown's Bright Horizons Family Solutions are systematic about measuring and maximizing their positive impact in their communities through charitable donations, mutually beneficial community partnerships, volunteer work, and more.

Academic learning—from elementary school to graduate programs—is being integrated with twenty-first-century skill building, emphasizing critical tools and entrepreneurial decision making needed for the future, real-world problem solving, and exposure of students to issues and dilemmas they are likely to encounter in the years to come. Suzanne McKechnie Klahr's BUILD in California (with recent expansion to Washington, D.C.), for example, is a non-profit that prepares urban students for college by helping them launch student-run organizations and providing them with professional mentors.

By breaking down the barriers separating learning and life, for-profit and non-profit, work and play, emerging generations are teaching us that life must not be relegated to disconnected silos. Rather, it can be lived coherently and fluidly, with our purpose, work, relationships, choice of place to live, and activities coming together powerfully in an integrated whole.

AN IMPROVISED MELODY

The spirit of life entrepreneurship is inspired by the freedom of living a life that is decidedly our own. Life entrepreneurs start with that as a foundation, bringing their lives back in line with their values and purpose. Rather than marching to someone else's drumbeat, they lead their own jazz band. With time and experience, they stop playing from a score and start improvising a new tune.

Part of that impulse comes from being dissatisfied with the status quo. As life entrepreneurs work to create a new future, they are transforming the way we work, learn, and live. In their untethered world, they pursue their dreams in unconventional ways. In honoring their authenticity, they hold fast to their values and purpose. In their integration of the various elements of their lives, they create playful melodies and elegant harmonies with others.

The two concluding stories that follow strike these chords, showing how three remarkable people have written their own score, overcome adversity, and discovered their authentic selves in the process. By bringing it all together and integrating their lives, they are now the change they wish to see in the world (to borrow a phrase from Mahatma Gandhi).

BEING THE CHANGE

From an early age, Bill George wanted to be a CEO. By the time he was thirty, he was president of Litton Microwave Cooking Products, growing their microwave business from $10 million to $200 million in sales. At thirty-eight, he became president of Honeywell's European division. Within three years, he became sector head. It turned out to be the "worst promotion I got in my life," he remarks. "I looked at myself in the mirror one day coming home and said, *I am miserable*. I realized I was trying to be someone I wasn't. I thought I was changing Honeywell to make it more dynamic but realized it was changing me." Upon deep personal reflection, he realized he wanted to be an "authentic" and values-based leader in a company that made a difference in people's lives.

At age forty-six he left the CEO track of Honeywell to join Medtronic, a much smaller pacemaker company out of Minneapolis that had previously tried recruiting him several times as CEO. "When I walked through the doors of Medtronic," he recalls, "I felt like I was coming home. That was a place I was meant to be all along, but I was too blind to see it because I was chasing my own ego."

He gave himself ten years to build a great company whose actions were always aligned with its values and mission to restore people to a full and healthy life. At Medtronic, he found kindred spirits who joined with him to create a collaborative culture that drew on their shared values and humanity, not just their commercial opportunities. By the time he stepped down, over seven million people's lives were being restored *every year* through Medtronic's medical devices (up from three hundred thousand a year when he started), and the company's market capitalization had grown from $1 billion to more than $60 billion. And they collaboratively created an inspiring work environment in the process.

Meanwhile, his wife, Penny George, had been working for various psychology consulting firms, where she counseled clients on their career path and other matters. "I loved the human stories," she recalls. "It was a ministry in a way—helping people identify what they really wanted to do with their lives."

Shortly after setting up a private practice, she was diagnosed with breast cancer. Her initial reaction was disbelief. "After that," Penny recalls, "there was a sense that all was lost and I was going to die." After a mastectomy, she underwent chemotherapy regimens for seven months, to be followed by years of hormonal therapy.

She soon discovered that "the medical system really didn't have anything to offer in terms of healing." In addition to a new diet, exercise, and stress reduction, she also tried a number of unconventional treatments: acupuncture, Chinese herbs, a healer, energy fields, and more. She also went on a vision quest—a Native American rite of passage—in the remote Four Corners area of the American Southwest.

These experiences transformed her sense of self and led her to a new calling: promoting integrative medicine. She explains,

> I grew up with the sense of medicine as a sacred calling. It was a covenant, not a contract. Medicine has gotten away from that. Now the system is broken. Being responsible for yourself is the ultimate primary care but also a source of transformation. It wasn't these therapies that I did that were transformative but the fact of taking responsibility and becoming the agent of my own life and not being a victim. . . . It wasn't until I got cancer that a whole new world opened up that brought together the ministry, the medicine, and the psychology—the mind, body, spirit part of healing. . . .
> I just knew that this was something I was giving myself to. It was a renewed sense of purpose in my life.

After supporting Penny through her crucible and marveling at how she reinvented herself, Bill began reflecting on his next chapter, particularly as he approached retirement. "My mission for this next phase of my life," he realized, "is to try to have some influence on leaders of the future." Today, he is doing that by championing authentic, ethical leadership and passing on leadership lessons via his books and his courses at Harvard University. When asked about the counsel he provides to his students, he says, "It's okay not to find the right fit in your profession right away, but you have to keep trying and never settle. When you find the right fit, everything changes. . . . You are never too young to think about the legacy you want to leave behind." Because Bill is at the vanguard of the shift toward authentic, values-based leadership in the business world, those words carry even greater weight with his young charges.

Bill and Penny recently launched a family foundation that focuses on making contributions to the fields that are their respective passions: leadership development and integrative medicine. Penny runs the foundation and also helped launch the Bravewell Collaborative, which unites philanthropists, health care providers, and consumers in the shared cause of improving health care. They have also created a travel schedule that allows them to spend quality time in the communities they value with the people they love, including building a house to spend time with their two sons and extended family in the mountains of Colorado. Their lives have now become abundantly untethered, with freedom to invent their work and days as they see fit. They have made authenticity a resounding theme that they live out loud, and they are integrating their life, work, marriage, parenting, and grandparenting into a happy and enriching whole. What's more, they are changing not only their own worlds but also ours through their writing, teaching, and evangelizing about causes that matter most to them.

In their Colorado home is a sculpture of a happy little girl on a swing being pushed by a little boy—a gift from Bill to Penny when she recovered from cancer. The little boy is Bill and the little girl is Penny. In many respects, the sculpture depicts their lives—the soaring freedom of swinging high into the air, the innocent authenticity of their play, and the joy of being together and loving one another, both looking ahead to the future.

THE RED RUBBER BALL

When Kevin Carroll was six, he and his brothers were abandoned by their mother in Virginia, packed up on a bus, and sent to live with their grandparents in Philadelphia. His grandmother passed away a few years later, leaving just his grandfather and the boys. He recalls that his grandfather would always ask him about his "want-to": "My pop-pop would say, 'How's your want-to today? You can't do anything with a broke want-to. You got to want-to be better. You got to want-to be different. You got to want-to be special. You got to want-to chase your dream.' He would always remind me, 'Make sure you check your want-to every day. '"

Kevin found his "want-to" in the local playground. He describes an encounter he had there one morning: "It was so early in the morning there were no children up there. I just was hanging out, and I saw a red rubber ball. I started to play for a little bit, and the next thing you know, kids started to come up to the playground, and they invited me in. They saw me with the ball, bouncing it around, and they just welcomed me. It was a watershed moment for me because I had never been so initially and unconditionally welcomed."

Though Kevin was the smallest of the bunch, he earned their respect through the fervor with which he played. He says, "I had to be a fighter. I learned how to fight and scratch and compete through sports. They called me 'little fast kid. '"

With nothing holding him back, Kevin had the run of the land. He spent much of his time just wandering around the streets. His scrappy attitude and animated spirit attracted the support of a surprising ensemble of adults. Kevin relates, "I got taught by winos, addicts, and dealers. I got doled out advice from any kind of wayward soul you could imagine. They'd say, 'You have to be two times better than anybody who's not of color. Two times better. How are you doing in your books?'"

His best friend's mom, Miss Lane, also became his mentor and second mother. As he explains,

> Miss Lane was the person who pushed and fought for me. I came home and said I was going to take vocational because that's what they told me. She said, "No, you're going to college." I asked her, "What do you think about me trying out for the Shakespeare play?" She says, "Well, why not?" Then I said, "They asked if we wanted to try a musical instrument and I'm thinking about trying something nobody else picked." She says, "Well, why not?" So there I am, playing the cello in the orchestra, doing Shakespeare, and the starting running back. Miss Lane was the person who gave me permission to dream as big as I wanted to dream.

And so he did. After high school, he signed up for the Air Force, telling the recruiter, "Give me the job that will get me out of here the fastest." That took him abroad, where he became a language instructor and interpreter and learned five languages.

After ten years of military service, he was ready to reengage his passion for sports. He returned to his old neighborhood and landed a job at the Haverford School as athletic trainer and physical education teacher, becoming the first person of color on the faculty there. Next, he became athletic trainer at St. Joseph's University, where the Philadelphia 76ers basketball team practiced. There he caught the attention of the Sixers coach, becoming the third African American head athletic trainer in the NBA's history.

Shortly thereafter, he was invited to speak at Nike's basketball camp to five hundred young athletes. "When I was a kid," he told them, "people said nothing good was going to happen to me.

And yet I stand here now as the head trainer for the Philadelphia 76ers. Anything is possible."

Given an opportunity to spend more time with his growing sons, Kevin accepted an open-ended job offer from Nike and became their "Katalyst" (a job that he invented to stimulate innovation throughout the global sporting goods corporation). There, he developed a wristband concept with motivational inscriptions that became the inspiration for the Lance Armstrong wristband phenomenon, now sixty-one million bands strong (and counting). After that he started his own business, wrote a book, became a motivational speaker, and started an international movement to get people tuned in to their dreams through the lessons of sports and play—all activities designed to translate his life story into a positive impact.

"The ball saved my life," he says now. "It gave me something to look forward to every day, something to literally chase. It was a way of changing my circumstances. . . . You've got to have something that you're inspired by and that you want to chase every day. You have to be able to answer the question, *What's your red rubber ball?*"

Kevin's story is inspirational and instructive. Here was a young boy who was almost entirely untethered at a precious young age, making him impressionable and vulnerable. Yet he was able to find grounding in an unlikely place: a playground. Recognizing and pursuing opportunities while honoring the lessons of influential mentors, Kevin built a life that was truly his own, infused with his passion for sports and play. Interestingly, he returned to an untethered life of sorts, creating a set of flexible work engagements that integrate all the things he loves: sports, play, being with his two sons, and encouraging young people. And it was all on his own terms. By discovering and embracing who he was, he was able to integrate his life in ways that delight and motivate others.

SAGE AND WARRIOR

The fifty-five stories of life entrepreneurs like Bill, Penny, and Kevin have much to teach us. They contain lessons about figuring out who we are, where we want to go, how we want to live, and what future we want to create. They are about embracing freedom, living authentically, and integrating the things that matter to us into a life of purpose and significance.

In the end, we see a powerful nexus where the entrepreneurial life meets the good life. There we see that we must become both sage and warrior: sage, in that we must be able to sit still long enough to discover purpose, get in tune with values, and dream up a vision that can illuminate our path forward; warrior, in that we must be driven by audacious goals, prepared for battle through strategy and resourcefulness, and willing—in the face of risk—to take decisive action that can carry the day.

The ancients talked about both the *vita activa,* a life of action, and the *vita contemplativa,* a life of reflection. Renowned psychologist Mihaly Czikszentmihalyi says, "Activity and reflection should ideally complement and support each other. Action by itself is blind, reflection impotent."[11] This interplay of reflection and action, of being and doing, affords us the opportunity to do remarkable things in the world and to imbue our lives with not only passion and joy but also meaning and significance.

When we realize that the dividing line between ordinary lives and extraordinary ones is mostly a fiction fueled by fear, inhibition, and failure of the imagination, we begin to see our lives in terms of possibility. There is no limit on the number of entrepreneurial lives that can be claimed. The elements of life entrepreneurship are open to all of us, not a select few. When we live this way, we bring light and hope to the world, for ourselves and for others.

The first and most important step in creating an extraordinary life is choosing to do so—with imagination, courage, and conviction. When it comes to integrating life, work, and purpose, we can do so with creativity, playfulness, and passion. Sometimes the hardest part of leading an entrepreneurial life is getting out of the way of the good life that wants to charge forth from within.

There are no guarantees of success, no suggestions of an easy ride. But there is limitless opportunity on this frontier— opportunity to connect with inspiring people and apply ourselves to worthy endeavors that test our mettle and shape our character.

There is freedom there—freedom to lead lives definitively of our own choosing. There is joy there—the kind that binds us together in adventures worthy of the lives we've been given. And there is grace—the overwhelming sense of beauty and wonder that can elevate our days.

> *In the time of your life, live.*
> —WILLIAM SAROYAN

Appendix A: Life Entrepreneurship Primer

This appendix presents the main points from *Life Entrepreneurs* for easy reference.

Patterns of Living

Seekers are looking for something more in life and find themselves wandering, yet are not quite sure where they want to end up. (high drive; low direction)	*Captains* have reflected deeply on where they want to go in life and have the drive to get there, actively steering in that direction. (high drive; high direction)
Drifters let the wind and waves take them where they will, going along for the ride. (low drive; low direction)	*Passengers* know where they wish to go in life but have not taken the action to get there. (low drive; high direction)

Key Take-Aways
- Both drive and direction are required. *Drive* is the motivation, desire, or willingness to do something—the fire in the belly that breathes life into everything we do and fuels our motivation to act and take risks. *Direction* is the harnessing force that channels our drive toward a desirable destination. Our direction comes from our core identity and gives us a sense of where we should be heading.
- These patterns of living occur on a continuum. Far from being set in stone, they are pliable and highly subject to our influence and will. We always retain the ability to change our life pattern.
- We can't always be captains in every facet of our lives. There are times in life for seeking, wandering, and even being passengers on someone else's ship.

- It isn't just about the one who is steering the ship. We travel our journey in life with others who are essential to the voyage.
- Drive is most likely to appear when we have a strong core identity of purpose and values and then deliberately choose activities that enliven us—and companions who uplift us.
- Direction is not a specific latitude and longitude. Rather, it is a broader horizon aligned with who we are and what we believe. It may take some time to discover through active seeking.

The Path of the Life Entrepreneur

Discovering Core Identity. Becoming acquainted with our authentic selves— especially our *values* and *purpose*—which are informed by our needs, strengths, and passions (internal), as well as our history, current circumstances, and relationships (external). These elements should inform but not dictate our path. We always have the ability to choose anew. In the end we must know ourselves deeply. This is not solely an inward journey—we also become acquainted with ourselves through relationships with others and our actions in the world.

> I have often thought that the best way to define a man's character is to seek out the particular mental or moral attitude in which, when it came upon him, he felt himself most deeply and intensively active and alive. At such moments, there is a voice inside which speaks and says, "This is the real me."
>
> —*William James*

Awakening to Opportunity. Being "switched on" to the world around us, assessing opportunities as they arise, and translating these kernels of recognition into actionable opportunities.

> All of us, whether or not we are warriors, have a cubic centimeter of chance that pops out in front of our eyes from time to time. The difference between an average man and a warrior is that the warrior is aware of this, and one of his tasks is to be alert, deliberately waiting, so that when his cubic centimeter pops out he has the necessary speed, the prowess, to pick it up.
>
> —*Carlos Castaneda*

Envisioning the Future. Developing a vivid description of who we will be and what we will do with our lives. Our vision is unearthed from within even as it is informed by opportunity and circumstance, reflecting a nexus of internal and external elements. With vivid clarity, our vision should raise our sights, inspiring us to something audacious and worthy of pursuit.

Fortune favors the audacious.

—*Desiderius Erasmus*

Developing Goals and Strategies. Goals and strategies provide needed clarity and focus to any entrepreneurial plan. Goals should be purposeful and prioritized, clear and measurable, and challenging but achievable. Once our goals are established, we can identify the gaps between our current reality and envisioned future and start planning to fill those gaps by leveraging existing resources and attracting new ones.

It must be borne in mind that the tragedy of life does not lie in not reaching your goals, the tragedy lies in not having any goals to reach.

—*Dr. Benjamin Isaiah Mays*

Building Healthy Support Systems. None of us can create a life of significance on our own. By reaching out to and developing trusting relationships with a diverse support network, we create opportunities for mutual benefit that reinforce one another based on the power of reciprocity (the positive network effect).

We are all angels with only one wing: we can only fly by embracing each other.

—*Luciano De Crescenzo*

Taking Action and Making a Difference. Summoning the courage to enter into the arena to bring our vision to life, finding ways to serve and contribute as we do so. The entrepreneur, by definition, is the acting person.

Nothing on earth is more gladdening than knowing we must roll up our sleeves and move back the boundaries of the humanly possible once again.

—*Annie Dillard*

Embracing Renewal and Reinvention. Stepping back and assessing where we have come from and where we are going, building in time for us to reconnect with our core identity and prepare for the journey ahead—and making wholesale changes in the fabric of our lives when necessary.

Yesterday is a wind gone down, a sun dropped in the west. I tell you that there is nothing in the world, only an ocean of tomorrows, a sky of tomorrow.

—*Carl Sandburg*

Reminders for the Road Ahead

- There are different routes to the trailhead of life entrepreneurship. We all find it in our own way and on our own timetable. Sometimes we take the long way. That's okay, as long as we eventually end up moving in the direction in which we want to go.
- Often we find the right path through a process of elimination, by trying things and ruling them out so we can figure out what we *don't* want to do.
- The right path is defined broadly: it tends to be a wider swath, a broader area of focus or themes of activity, as opposed to a single trail in the forest with our name written on it.
- The path is winding and usually makes sense only in retrospect. We must plan as best we can and be purposeful as we walk it, but life always surprises.
- Finding the right path is one of the most important things we can do in life, and we should keep at it until we do.

When we walk the path with all of these elements, we find that:

- They give our lives meaning.
- They are open to all of us and exist in unlimited supply.

How to Walk the Path

Authentic Integrity. Integration of all aspects of our lives in a way that coheres with our true nature, flowing from our core identity (purpose and values).

Deep Awareness. Being alert to who we are and the changing needs, challenges, and opportunities that surround us.

Breakthrough Innovation. Game-changing, applied creativity that helps us transcend the boundaries of the present.

Courage to Try. An openness to act in spite of our fears and a predisposition toward going for it.

Purposeful Spontaneity. A willingness to let go, improvise, and seize new opportunities in a way that resonates with our deepest essence and reason for being.

Adaptive Persistence. Tailoring our approach to the circumstances while persevering through adversity.

Pervasive Service. An ethic of contribution as a defining feature of our lives.

- They require that we pay attention to how we are living.
- They insist that we take the long view.
- They encourage that we be both warrior and sage, alternating between action and reflection.
- They add up to a life of adventure, fulfillment, service, and significance.
- They build toward our legacy.

> *Here's what I wanted to tell you today: get a life. A real life, not a manic pursuit. . . . Get a life in which you are not alone. . . . Get a life in which you are generous. . . . Care so deeply about its goodness that you want to spread it around. . . . It is so easy to waste our lives: our days, our hours, our minutes. . . . It is so easy to exist instead of live.*
> —ANNA QUINDLEN

APPENDIX B: EXERCISES AND HELPFUL RESOURCES

We wrote this book to inspire action as well as reflection. For those interested in applying the principles of life entrepreneurship to your life, we have developed a full array of exercises and compiled a library of helpful resources that directly complement the ideas, findings, and themes of this book.

The exercises include:

- Assessing personal drive and direction
- Discovering core identity:

  Needs, passions, strengths
  History, relationships, current circumstances
  Values and purpose

- Recognizing and assessing opportunity
- Creating a vision statement
- Setting clear and measurable goals
- Developing strategies
- Mapping and building healthy support systems
- Taking action
- Embracing renewal and reinvention
- Developing an "entrepreneurial life plan"

These exercises can be found at **www.lifeentrepreneurs.com**.

On the site you will also find:

- More information on the people we interviewed
- Additional profiles of life entrepreneurs
- Life entrepreneurship assessments

- Opportunities to connect with other life entrepreneurs
- Other helpful information and features, such as relevant articles, organizations, and websites, a suggested reading list, and more

Take a look and let us know what you think. We look forward to continuing the conversation.

Appendix C: Interview Methodology

Interviews for this book were conducted with people deemed by the authors to be life entrepreneurs—that is, people who create lives of significance through opportunity recognition, innovation, and action—including both business and social entrepreneurs. All interviews were conducted by Christopher Gergen, Gregg Vanourek, or both between September 2005 and June 2007. In a few cases, two people were interviewed together (for example, business partners and entrepreneurial couples). Some interviews were conducted in person, others by phone. The interviews generally lasted between sixty and ninety minutes. All interviews were recorded with the permission of the interviewee (mostly by audio but in a few cases by video). Interviews were subsequently transcribed and analyzed.

The interviewers used a common set of questions but allowed the interview conversation to be guided based on the experiences and interests of the interviewees. In several cases, time did not allow asking the full range of questions. A typical interview covered the following subjects:

- Personal background: life narrative and early influences
- Entrepreneurial and life experiences, including

  Recognizing opportunities
  Developing a vision
  Goal setting and strategy development
  Resourcefulness and building personal support systems
  Taking action

- Lessons learned through entrepreneurial and life experiences:

  Challenges and failures
  Perceptions of risk
  Renewal strategies
  Suggestions for aspiring life entrepreneurs

Time permitting, additional questions were asked about courage, purpose, values, life balance and integration, decision making, drive and direction, spontaneity, service, adaptation and persistence, entrepreneurial pitfalls, and legacy.

In total, fifty-five people were interviewed. Attention was paid to ensuring diversity of gender, race and ethnicity, geography, age, generation, sector (for-profit, non-profit, and public), and industry, as demonstrated by the following:

- Thirty-three percent of the interviewees were female.
- Fifteen percent were racial or ethnic minorities (nonwhite).
- Eleven percent were born outside the United States.
- Thirty-eight percent have had professional experience outside of the United States.
- Seventy-eight percent had previously been engaged in business entrepreneurship, and 51 percent had been engaged in social entrepreneurship (the total exceeds 100 percent because some people were involved with both).
- Interviewees have worked across a wide range of industries, including biotechnology, consulting, education, entertainment, food service, government, health and medicine, law, military, philanthropy, politics, ranching, religion, sports, and technology.

NOTES

Introduction

1. Gregg Easterbrook, *The Progress Paradox: How Life Gets Better While People Feel Worse* (New York: Random House, 2003), 164.
2. Source: Society for Human Resource Management, www.shrm.org; Conference Board, www.conference-board.org (accessed July 26, 2007).
3. Claudia Wallis, "The New Science of Happiness," *Time*, January 17, 2005.
4. Paul H. Ray and Sherry Ruth Anderson, *The Cultural Creatives: How 50 Million People Are Changing the World* (New York: Three Rivers Press, 2001).
5. Source: www.whatsyourmotto.com/AboutUs.aspx (accessed August 1, 2007).

Chapter One

1. Daniel H. Pink, *Free Agent Nation: The Future of Working for Yourself* (New York: Business Plus, 2001), 14, 40, and 41.
2. An *intrapreneur* is defined as a person within a large corporation who takes direct responsibility for turning an idea into a profitable finished product through assertive risk taking and innovation (*American Heritage Dictionary*). Source: http://dictionary.reference.com/browse/intrapreneur (accessed July 24, 2007).
3. Jody Miller and Matt Miller, "The New Human-Sized Job," *Fortune*, November 29, 2005.
4. Jim Phills, "15 Minutes: Kevin Johnson," *Stanford Social Innovation Review*, Spring 2007, 25–27.
5. For an excellent account of Aristotle's writing and thinking on the good life, see James O'Toole, *Creating the Good Life: Applying Aristotle's Wisdom to Find Meaning and Happiness* (New York: Rodale, 2005).
6. Richard Leider and David Shapiro, *Repacking Your Bags: How to Live with a New Sense of Purpose* (New York: Barnes & Noble Books, 1996), 26, 32.

Chapter Two

1. Gary Erickson with Lois Lorentzen, *Raising the Bar: Integrity and Passion in Life and Business* (San Francisco: Jossey-Bass, 2004), 30–32. All quotes are from our interview with Gary Erickson unless otherwise indicated.
2. Ibid., 318.
3. Ibid., 26.
4. Ibid., 266.
5. Ibid., 174, 239.

Chapter Three

1. The short list we have compiled as evidence of this, with the help of others, includes the following: the Oracle at Delphi, Lao Tzu, Buddhism, Jesus Christ, Muhammad, Hasidic Judaism, Chaucer, Kierkegaard, Emerson, and Michael Pastore. Many of the examples in this listing come from Kevin Cashman, *Leadership from the Inside Out: Becoming a Leader for Life* (Minneapolis: TCLG, 1998), 120.
2. Bill George with Peter Sims, *True North: Discover Your Authentic Leadership* (San Francisco: Jossey-Bass, 2007), xxiii.
3. Christina Baldwin, *Storycatcher: Making Sense of Our Lives Through the Power of Story* (Novato, CA: New World Library, 2005).
4. Kevin Cashman, *Leadership from the Inside Out,* 51.
5. Bill George with Peter Sims, *True North,* xxviii.
6. Source: James O'Toole, *Creating the Good Life: Applying Aristotle's Wisdom to Find Meaning and Happiness* (New York: Rodale Books, 2005), 175.
7. See Ronald Heifetz and Marty Linsky, *Leadership on the Line* (Cambridge, MA: Harvard Business Review Press, 2002).
8. Bill George, *Authentic Leadership: Rediscovering the Secrets to Creating Lasting Value* (San Francisco: Jossey-Bass, 2003), 14–15.
9. Albert Wiseman, Donald Clifton, and Curt Liesveld, *Living Your Strengths: Discovering Your God-Given Talents and Inspire Your Community* (New York: Gallup Press, 2004), ix–x, 3, 8. They also define *strengths* as "the ability to provide consistent, near-perfect performance." The authors define a *talent* as a naturally recurring pattern of thought, feeling, or behavior that can be productively applied; a *skill* as an ability to perform the steps of an activity, which can be learned; and *knowledge* as what you know—which can be either factual or experiential knowledge (4–6).
10. Tom Rath, "The Fallacy Behind the American Dream," *Gallup Management Journal,* February 8, 2007, http://gml.gallup.com (accessed April 2, 2007).

11. Marcus Buckingham cited in J. J. Smith, "Buckingham: Focus on Strengths, Not Weaknesses," Society for Human Resource Management, *HR News*, March 23, 2007.

12. Source: Michael Kaplan, "How to Overcome Your Strengths," *Fast Company*, April 1999, 224.

13. Jerry Porras, Stewart Emery, and Mark Thompson, *Success Built to Last: Creating a Life That Matters* (New Jersey: Wharton School Publishing, 2007), 35.

14. Curt Rosengren, "Right Reality: Find Your Passion Compass," *The Wag*, November 10, 2006.

15. Laura Nash and Howard Stevenson, "Success That Lasts," *Harvard Business Review*, February 2004, 32; see also Laura Nash and Howard Stevenson, *Just Enough: Tools for Creating Success in Your Work and Life* (Hoboken, NJ: Wiley, 2004).

16. These examples of possible values were taken, with permission, from a list from a Vail Leadership Institute exercise (see www.vailleadership.org).

17. Donald Sull and Dominic Houlder, "Do Your Commitments Match Your Convictions?" *Harvard Business Review*, January 2005, 22–23.

18. Jim Collins summarizing his book *Built to Last* (coauthored with Jerry Porras; New York: HarperCollins, 1997) in "Built to Flip," *Fast Company*, February 2000, 32, 131.

19. Richard Leider, *The Power of Purpose: Creating Meaning in Your Life and Work* (San Francisco: Berrett-Koehler, 1997), 2.

20. Ibid.

Chapter Four

1. Paul Lemberg, "Six Ways to Get Out of a Rut," *Nonprofit World*, July/August 2006, 18.

2. Martin Seligman, *Learned Optimism: How to Change Your Mind and Your Life* (New York: Vintage Books, 2006), 15.

3. Ibid.

4. Robert Roy Britt, "Study: Optimists Live Longer," *LiveScience*, November 1, 2004, www.livescience.com (accessed February 27, 2007).

5. Carol Dweck, *Mindset: The New Psychology of Success* (New York: Random House, 2006).

6. Ellen Langer, *Mindfulness* (Cambridge, MA: DeCapo Press, 1989).

7. Peter Guber in "My Greatest Lesson," *Fast Company*, May 1998, 83.

8. Peter Drucker, *Innovation and Entrepreneurship* (New York: HarperCollins, 1985), 19–30.

9. Most of Richard's story comes from his interview with the authors. Other source: Curt Rosengren, "Spring Board," *Motto*, May/June 2007, 61–65.

10. Barry Schwartz, *The Paradox of Choice: Why More Is Less* (New York: HarperCollins, 2004).

11. Most of Kimberly's story comes from her interview with the authors. Other sources: Jackie Kucinich, "Yoga Instructor Making a Splash in D.C.," *The Hill*, February 26, 2004; Danaline Bryant, "City Native Finds Her Muse," *Sunday Constitution*, October 3, 2004; Women's Business Center, "WBC Success Story: Kimberly Wilson," www.tranquilspace.com (accessed January 4, 2007).

Chapter Five

1. Source: Example taken from Jim Collins and Jerry Porras, "Building Your Company's Vision," *Harvard Business Review*, September/October 2006.

2. Source: Bureau of Transportation Statistics (www.bts.gov/publications/national_transportation_statistics), accessed July 27, 2007.

3. Source: Evoca website (www.evoca.com), accessed July 27, 2007.

4. We used Evoca to conduct and record many of the phone-based interviews for this book.

5. Source: U.S. Constitution Online site (http://www.usconstitution.net/dream.html), accessed July 27, 2007.

6. According to Jim Collins and Jerry Porras, one of the key components of a vision is an "envisioned future" (which also needs to be tied into our purpose and values, which they call "core ideology"). Our envisioned future is "what we aspire to become, to achieve, and to create—something that will require significant change and progress to attain." It comprises (1) a vision-level, ten to thirty-year big, hairy, audacious goal ("BHAG"); and (2) a vivid description: "a vibrant, engaging, and specific description of what it would be like to achieve the BHAG." Jim Collins and Jerry Porras, "Building Your Company's Vision," *Harvard Business Review*, September–October 2006.

7. Daniel Gilbert, *Stumbling on Happiness* (New York: Knopf, 2006), 4.

8. Ibid., 112.

9. S. A. Newcomb, *Side-Lights on Astronomy* (New York: Harper & Brothers, 1906), 355.

10. Gilbert, *Stumbling on Happiness*, 114.

11. Source: Chipotle's website: http://www.chipotle.com (accessed July 27, 2007).

12. Howard Schultz quote in Bill George with Peter Sims, *True North: Discover Your Authentic Leadership* (San Francisco: Jossey-Bass, 2007), 7.
13. Source: www.starbucks.com (accessed July 27, 2007).

Chapter Six

1. Amar Bhide, "The Questions Every Entrepreneur Must Answer," *Harvard Business Review*, November 1996.
2. Jim Collins, "Turning Goals into Results: The Power of Catalytic Mechanisms," *Harvard Business Review*, February 2000.
3. See Marshall Goldsmith and Kelly Goldsmith, "The Five Reasons We Give Up," *Business Week*, January 24, 2007.
4. George Leonard, *Mastery: The Keys to Success and Long-Term Fulfillment* (New York: Plume, 1992), 140.
5. Carl von Clausewitz quoted in Richard Luecke, *Strategy: Create and Implement the Best Strategy for Your Business* (Boston: Harvard Business School Press, 2005), xi.
6. "Mastering the context" is a term we are borrowing from Warren Bennis, *On Becoming a Leader* (New York: Basic Books, 2003), 6.
7. Herminia Ibarra, "How to Stay Stuck in the Wrong Career," *Harvard Business Review*, December 2002.
8. Richard Pascale quoted in Alan Webber, "How Business Is a Lot Like Life," *Fast Company*, March 2001, 130.
9. Ayse Guclu, J. Gregory Dees, and Beth B. Anderson, "The Process of Social Entrepreneurship: Creating Opportunities Worthy of Serious Pursuit," Center for the Advancement of Social Entrepreneurship, Duke University, November 2002, 10.
10. Source: Endeavor's website: http://www.endeavor.org (accessed July 27, 2007). Note that the entrepreneurs they have invested in include Leila Velez in Brazil and Natalie Kilassy in South Africa, both featured in this book.

Chapter Seven

1. Jim Erickson, "Plan to Save Aspen," *Rocky Mountain News*, September 11, 2006.
2. James O'Toole, *Creating the Good Life: Applying Aristotle's Wisdom to Find Meaning and Happiness* (New York: Rodale Books, 2005), 174–176.
3. Sources: *Reinventing Aging: Baby Boomers and Civic Engagement*, Harvard School of Public Health—MetLife Foundation, 2004; Ichiro Kawachi, "Long Live Community: Social Capital as Public Health," *Prospect*, November–December 1997; Stewart Powell,

"Retirees Can Prolong Life by Volunteering, Study Says," *Deseret News*, June 17, 2004; Nancy Weaver Teichert, "Volunteer for a Longer, Happier Life," *Sacramento Bee*, July 7, 2004; Winnie Yip et al., "Does Social Capital Enhance Health and Well-Being? Evidence from Rural China," *Social Science and Medicine*, 2007, *64*, 35–49.

4. Robert Putnam, *Bowling Alone: The Collapse and Revival of American Community* (New York: Simon & Schuster, 2001).

5. Sebastian Mallaby, "Why So Lonesome?" *Washington Post*, June 26, 2006, A21.

6. Eric Liu, *Guiding Lights: The People Who Lead Us Toward Our Purpose in Life* (New York: Random House, 2004).

7. Carl Schramm, *The Entrepreneurial Imperative: How America's Economic Miracle Will Reshape the World (and Change Your Life)* (New York: HarperCollins, 2006), 174.

8. Randy Komisar, "Goodbye Career, Hello Success," *Harvard Business Review*, March–April 2000.

9. Source: James Kouzes and Barry Posner, *The Leadership Challenge* (San Francisco: Jossey-Bass, 1995).

10. Michael Copeland, "Social Networking Has Been Great with the Kids, but Not of Much Use to Business—Until Now," *Business 2.0*, February 28, 2007.

11. Stephen R. Covey, *The Seven Habits of Highly Effective People: Powerful Lessons in Personal Change* (New York: Free Press, 1989, 2004).

12. Stephen M. R. Covey, *The Speed of Trust: The One Thing That Changes Everything* (New York: Free Press, 2006).

13. Brian Uzzi and Shannon Dunlap, "How to Build Your Network," *Harvard Business Review*, December 2005.

Chapter Eight

1. See also Joseph Jaworski, *Synchronicity: The Inner Path of Leadership* (San Francisco: Berrett-Koehler, 1996).

2. Tom Peters, "Tom Peters's True Confessions," *Fast Company*, November 2001, Issue 53, 78.

3. Bill Shore, *The Cathedral Within: Transforming Your Life by Giving Something Back* (New York: Random House, 1999).

4. Honest Tea website: http://www.honesttea.com (accessed June 25, 2007).

5. Information in this profile of Seth Goldman comes mostly from our interview with him but also from the Harvard Business School case (9–201–076), "Honest Tea," by Paul G. Gompers, October 17,

2001, as well as the Honest Tea website, http://www.honesttea.com (accessed June 25, 2007).

6. John McCain, "In Search of Courage: Finding the Courage Within You," *Fast Company*, September 2004, 56.

Chapter Nine

1. John W. Gardner, *Living, Leading, and the American Dream* (San Francisco: Jossey-Bass, 2003).
2. Source: William C. Taylor and Polly LaBarre, *Mavericks at Work* (New York: Morrow, 2006).
3. Stephen R. Covey, *The Seven Habits of Highly Effective People: Powerful Lessons in Personal Change* (New York: Free Press, 1989, 2004).
4. Source: Herbert Benson and Robert L. Allen, "How Much Stress Is Too Much?" *Harvard Business Review, 58,* 1980.
5. Edward M. Hallowell, *Crazy Busy: Overstretched, Overbooked, and About to Snap!* (New York: Ballantine Books, 2006).
6. Source: Jim Loehr and Tony Schwartz, "The Making of a Corporate Athlete," *Harvard Business Review,* January 2001.
7. Ibid.
8. Source: Kevin Cashman, *Leadership from the Inside Out: Becoming a Leader for Life* (Minneapolis: TCLG, 1998).
9. Source: Lisa Belkin, "Life's Work: Some Respect, Please, for the American Nap," *New York Times,* February 25, 2007.
10. Source: Kay Redfield Jamison, *Exuberance: The Passion for Life* (New York: Knopf, 2004).
11. Donald N. Sull and Dominic Houlder, "Do Your Commitments Match Your Convictions?" *Harvard Business Review,* January 2005.
12. Leider also talks about the natural progression from the "warrior stage of leadership," focused on ambition, accomplishment, and advancement, to the "elder stage of leadership," focused on caring for, serving, and empowering others. See Richard Leider, *The Power of Purpose: Creating Meaning in Your Life and Work* (San Francisco: Berrett-Koehler, 1997).
13. Source: Charles Fishman, "Sabbaticals Are Serious Business," *Fast Company,* October 1996, 44.
14. Source: Christine Larson, "Time Out," *U.S. News & World Report,* February 28, 2005, EE2–EE8.
15. Warren Bennis and Robert Thomas, *Geeks and Geezers: How Era, Values, and Defining Moments Shape Leaders* (Boston: Harvard Business Press, 2002), 99.
16. Victor Frankl, *Man's Search for Meaning* (New York: Pocket Books, 1984).

17. Ibid.
18. Source: Anne Field, "A Living or a Life?" *Fast Company*, December 1999, 256. See also Mark Albion, *Making a Life, Making a Living: Reclaiming Your Purpose and Passion in Business and in Life* (New York: Warner Books, 2000).

Conclusion

1. Diane Ackerman, *A Natural History of the Senses* (London: Vintage, 1991).
2. Carl Schramm, *The Entrepreneurial Imperative: How America's Economic Miracle Will Reshape the World (and Change Your Life)* (New York: HarperCollins, 2006), 11, 49, 78.
3. Global Entrepreneurship Monitor Report 2002 cited in Richard Breeden, "Older Can Mean Better in Small-Business Owners," *Wall Street Journal*, August 20, 2002, http://online.wsj.com/article/SB1029787433237176275.html (accessed July 10, 2007).
4. *The Entrepreneur Next Door: Characteristics of Individuals Starting Companies in America, an Executive Summary of the Panel Study of Entrepreneurial Dynamics 2002*, Ewing Marion Kauffman Foundation, 14.
5. Robert Fairlie, *Kauffman Index of Entrepreneurial Activity, 1996–2006*, Ewing Marion Kauffman Foundation, 1.
6. Michael Selz, "Survey Finds 37% of Households Involved in Small-Business Arena," *Wall Street Journal*, December 13, 1996. http://online.wsj.com/article/SB850434701725909000.html (accessed July 10, 2007).
7. Global Entrepreneurship Monitor Report 2005, cited in "Globally, 41% of Entrepreneurs Are Women," *Wall Street Journal*, March 9, 2005.
8. Study cited by Kate Fox, *Coming of Age in the eBay Generation: Life Shopping and the New Life Skills in the Age of eBay*, Social Issues Research Centre, U.K., 2005, 5.
9. Holly Bull, "The Possibilities of the Gap Year," *Chronicle of Higher Education*, July 7, 2006.
10. Richard Florida captured this trend in his books, *The Rise of the Creative Class: And How It's Transforming Work, Leisure, Community, and Everyday Life* (New York: Basic Books, 2003) and *Flight of the Creative Class: The New Global Competition for Talent* (New York: HarperCollins, 2007).
11. Mihaly Czikszentmihalyi, *Flow: The Psychology of Optimal Experience* (New York: HarperPerennial, 1990), 226.

THE AUTHORS

Christopher Gergen is a founding partner of New Mountain Ventures (www.newountainventures.com), an entrepreneurial leadership development company. Additionally, Christopher is the cofounder and chairman of SMARTHINKING, the leading online tutoring provider in the United States—serving over two hundred thousand students from more than a thousand universities, colleges, and high schools. His other entrepreneurial ventures include starting a coffeehouse-bar dedicated to promoting the arts and music in Santiago, Chile, and helping to launch the Entrepreneur Corps—a national service initiative sponsored by AmeriCorps* VISTA that placed four hundred full-time business volunteers for a year of service in over ninety non-profit organizations across the country. Christopher is also the founder of LEAD!, a leadership, entrepreneurship, and service program for high school students at Gonzaga College High School in Washington, D.C., and he is a founding board member of E. L. Haynes Public Charter School.

Further professional experience includes serving as vice president of new market development for K12 Inc. and as chief operating officer and vice president of business development and strategy for New American Schools. Christopher received a bachelor of arts degree with honors from Duke University, a master's degree in public policy from George Washington University, and an M.B.A. from Georgetown University. Christopher is currently a visiting lecturer and director of the Entrepreneurial Leadership Initiative at Duke University within the Terry Sanford Institute of Public Policy's Hart Leadership Program. He lives with his wife and two children in Washington, D.C.

Gregg Vanourek is a founding partner of New Mountain Ventures and former CEO of Vanourek Consulting Solutions. Previously, Vanourek served as senior vice president of school development for K12 Inc., where he led the company's business and school development efforts and helped launch the company during its start-up. During his tenure at K12, Gregg led the team that launched and managed eight statewide virtual schools with over one hundred employees. Previously, he served as vice president for programs for the Thomas B. Fordham Foundation, where he helped to launch a private scholarship program for low-income youth in Dayton, Ohio. Before that, Gregg was a research fellow at the Hudson Institute, a leading national think tank.

Gregg has coauthored a book on charter schools (*Charter Schools in Action: Renewing Public Education,* published by Princeton University Press). He has also written several national education reports and book chapters, as well as dozens of articles for leading newspapers across the country. Gregg holds an M.B.A. from the Yale School of Management, a master of science degree from the London School of Economics, and a bachelor of arts degree from Claremont McKenna College. Gregg lives with his wife and daughter in Colorado, where he also serves on the board of the Vail Leadership Institute.

ACKNOWLEDGMENTS

The seeds for this book were sown in Warren Bennis and President Steve Sample's "Art of Leadership" class at the University of Southern California. Over several years we were urged to turn our words and stories about life entrepreneurship into a book. As a result, we owe Warren, Steve, and multiple cohorts of USC students a debt of gratitude. Warren, in particular, deserves singular credit for this book. His early encouragement, ongoing mentorship, introductions to Jossey-Bass, and suggestions for improvement have all been invaluable.

Once the book was under way, scores of people provided helpful guidance and constructive advice to help get it over the finish line. We are particularly grateful to those who provided us with specific feedback on early drafts and chapters, including Beth Anderson, Mark Barnett, David Gergen, David Gray, Jael Kampfe, Brint Markle, Andrew Park, Mike Petrilli, Peter Sims, and Bob Vanourek. Their ideas and insights made for a dramatically better book. In addition, we benefited from research assistance provided by Kent Grasso and Jeanne MacDonald as well as the diligent professionalism of Karen Notgarnie in her transcriptions of many of the interviews. Special thanks also to Murem Sharpe and Evoca for use of its phone-to-Web audio recording and transcription services—a great tool that helped us immensely. Shari Kowalski is also owed great thanks for staying on top of our accounts.

Our friends at Jossey-Bass deserve a lot of credit for turning hundreds of pages into a sharply focused and beautifully presented book. Special thanks are owed to Susan Williams (herself an inspired life entrepreneur) as well as Rob Brandt, Amy Packard, Amie Wong, Rebecca Browning, Carolyn Miller Carlstroem, Mark Karmendy, and our all-star copyeditor Kristi

Hein. Further thanks are owed to all of the people who agreed to be interviewed for this book and whose personal stories help this book shine—and who serve as personal inspirations to us. Without them this book would have been a pale shadow of what it is.

Christopher would like to offer special thanks to Eric, Lucy, Gus, and Ella Meyer, who provided much-needed and very welcome distraction, and Lowell Weiss and Sara Finkelstein for helping wrestle over the title and providing much-needed perspective on the book-writing process. The opportunity to teach the concepts embedded in this book has also been a great joy. As such, great thanks are extended to my colleagues, friends, and students at Duke University's Sanford Institute of Public Policy's Hart Leadership Program and Gonzaga College High School—as well as the wonderful teachers like Bruce Payne and Peter Cicchino who opened my eyes to the power of social change through entrepreneurial leadership.

Gregg would like to thank Miguel Brookes and Anne Marie Yarwood for memorable evenings spent wrestling with these ideas over a pint of beer or two. Richard Leider's work and writing have been seminal, and the thought leadership and friendship of John Horan-Kates of the Vail Leadership Institute have been deeply influential. Checker Finn has been a cherished mentor, not only in education and writing but also in life. Thanks to Steve Smith for a creative and authoritative introduction to "theories of the good life." John Roth has been a teacher and guide whose lessons grow richer and more present through the years.

We would also like to express our deepest gratitude to our families. This was a long, hard process. Our parents, Bob and June Vanourek and David and Anne Gergen, provided valued emotional support, exceptional counsel, insightful wisdom, and enduring love every step of the way. Similarly, our siblings and their partners, Katherine and Mark Barnett as well as Scott and Lori Vanourek, gave us big boosts when we most needed them (as well as definitive proof of the power of entrepreneurial couples).

Our own life partners, Heather and Kristina, helped spark this book at its inception, coached us through the challenges, remained patient with our obsessions over this labor of love, helped us celebrate the day we penned the very last lines, and renewed our passion for enthusiastically putting the lessons of this book to work in our own lives. Words could never describe our thanks to them.

Finally, to our young children—Alexandra and Maya (and her "little brother" on the way)—this book is really for you. We wrote this book with open hearts entrusted irrevocably to you. We ask only that you find it within yourselves to add richly to this unfolding story.

Warm regards,
Christopher and Gregg

INDEX